Friedrich Schleiermacher

DIALECTIC

or,
THE ART OF DOING PHILOSOPHY

AMERICAN ACADEMY OF RELIGION
TEXTS AND TRANSLATIONS SERIES

Edited by

Terry Godlove
Hofstra University

Number 11

Friedrich Schleiermacher
DIALECTIC

Translated, with Introduction and Notes by
Terrence N. Tice

Friedrich Schleiermacher

DIALECTIC

or,

THE ART OF DOING PHILOSOPHY

A Study Edition of the 1811 Notes

Translated, with Introduction and Notes by
Terrence N. Tice

Scholars Press
Atlanta, Georgia

Friedrich Schleiermacher

DIALECTIC

or,

THE ART OF DOING PHILOSOPHY

A Study Edition of the 1811 Notes

Translated, with Introduction and Notes by
Terrence N. Tice

Many thanks to Felix Meiner Verlag for their permission to publish excerpts.

Copyright ©1996
The American Academy of Religion

Library of Congress Cataloging in Publication Data
Schleiermacher, Friedrich, 1768–1834.
 [Dialektik. English]
 Dialectic, or, The art of doing philosophy : a study edition of the
1811 notes / Friedrich Schleiermacher ; translated, with introduction
and notes, by Terrence N. Tice.
     p.   cm. — (Texts and translations series / American Academy
of Religion ; no. 11)
 Includes bibliographical references (p.   ) and indexes.
 ISBN 0-7885-0293-X (paper : alk. paper)
 1. Dialectic. 2. Logic. I. Tice, Terrence N. II. Title.
III. Series: Texts and translations series (American Academy of Religion) ;
no. 11.
B3093.D52E5   1996
110—dc20   96-26529
                                                        CIP

Printed in the United States of America
on acid-free paper

Dedicated to
Sergio Sorrentino

TABLE OF CONTENTS

PREFACE

This study edition presents the first of Schleiermacher's eight forays into the foundations of all thinking that aims at knowing. It comprises the first translation of his "dialectic" into English. All the major themes are struck here, though in the next two decades arguments, explications and refinements of interest were added to these preparatory notes for Summer Term 1811. The Jonas text (1839) is used, plus some additions provided by Arndt (1986), by permission.

Schleiermacher had just begun to put all this material together for publication when his life was cut short in February 1834. Otherwise he would probably have destroyed all his notes, as he did with other such projects. This small section of the entire 610–page edition by Ludwig Jonas in the collected works (1839), I have found, offers a remarkably apt introduction to his views, especially as accompanied by editorial notes and commentary. It also stands on its own as a mature achievement in Schleiermacher's forty-second year. Before long, an English edition of all this material by Joseph Eckenrode and myself will be available for those who wish to explore these metaphysical/methodological inquiries into "the art of doing philosophy" further. It is to appear in the Schleiermacher: Studies and Translations series published by Edwin Mellen Press.

In recent years increasing interest has arisen in how this great founder of modern theology and of the modern study of religion thought about such matters, for in striking ways he has also been emerging as a notable philosopher for our own times. Thus, it is fitting that this seminal work should be released for use in many fields under auspices of the American Academy of Religion, which represents Schleiermacher's home field. My companion volume on Schleiermacher's "hermeneutics" is to appear in 1997 under the same aegis.

All the headings have been added, though the lecture numbers themselves were given in Schleiermacher's original manuscript.

I want to extend special thanks to David Klemm of the University of Iowa, who got me started on this project, and to Germanist Edwina Lawler of Drew University, who as always made numerous helpful suggestions, also to Ann Wood Schmitt, who expertly achieved the final word processing and formatting.

Terrence N. Tice
Estes Park, Colorado—August 1995
Ann Arbor, Michigan—March 1996

EDITOR'S INTRODUCTION

Friedrich Schleiermacher (1768–1834) was, among other things, the first, classic translator of Plato's works into German, a wide-ranging, original philosopher, including inquiry into the nature of the sciences and of the university as a special locus for scientific work, co-founder of the University of Berlin, founder of the modern study of religion, and father of the modern era in theology (for the last of which he has been chiefly known until recent decades). For him, philosophy plays crucial roles in all such activity. "Dialectic," the title he gave to several sets of lectures that he offered at the University of Berlin from 1811, within a year of its founding, to 1831, he simply defined as "the art of doing philosophy," or alternately as an investigation into the principles of knowing. This presentation is far more general in its scope than the usual contemporary theories of knowledge, which tend to address issues about how to obtain justified true belief and the like.

Already in its first form, as succinct preparatory notes for his 1811 lectures, his dialectic is well worth studying today. This is so not simply because they comprise a seminal work at what was arguably the outset of the modern age but also because they contain reflections that offer fresh challenges and contributions to scholarly efforts today—indeed, to the very notion of what it should mean to be a scholar, one who purports both to know and to understand how to get to the point of knowing. From the very beginning, he continually raises questions about the status of that which one may purport to know, the question as to the nature of "being" to which knowing refers, and about the status of "thinking" with the aim of knowing. In this way he leads us back to the general roots of all inquiry.

An Approach to Reading the 1811 Preparatory Notes

Much that might have gone into an introduction here has instead been placed in editorial notes and commentaries, where they are likely to do more good. The indexes are designed to help the reader have ready access to various concepts and other matters of interest.

Now, imagine, if you will, that in 1811 you had intended to take a course of lectures on the art of doing philosophy with Schleiermacher but could not attend at the 5:00 to 6:00 p.m. hour (63 others did, requiring the University's largest hall, except for halls in the Medical School). Many years after the course had ended, you came upon Schleiermacher's set of mostly preparatory notes for all but the first eleven of forty-nine hours, Monday to Wednesday from April 22 to late August in Summer Term. Luckily, in the same sheaf were summary notes especially for the first eleven hours by a highly astute young scholar named August Twesten, along with some further elaborations that Twesten carefully constructed based on these notes and with a conclusion he supplied for the entire series. Suppose, too, that someone certified to you that Twesten's various notes and comments were highly accurate, given a close knowledge of Schleiermacher's thinking and in comparison with summaries, made by Ludwig Jonas, who had been appointed by Schleiermacher to edit his lectures, from a student's transcript of the 1811 lectures, now lost. This is the situation you now face in attempting to think after Schleiermacher, assisted by these further aids, as to what he said at that time.

Suppose, in addition, that you had become quite intrigued about these lectures, because you learned that they highlighted a particular form of thinking that has the aim of "knowing" and that Schleiermacher saw this process, which was supposed to underlie and suffuse all sciences, as essentially dialogical. You had also learned that he applied the word "dialectic" to this process of thinking to produce knowing, in distinction from other kinds of thinking, so as to reflect something of the conversational and disputational qualities that were characteristic of ways in which early Greek philosophers worked out their ideas. You had been informed that Schleiermacher's recommendations for this kind of discourse, whether oral or in writing, reflected a highly open-minded style. This style is built on the awareness that all such thinking is in some way context-bound and tentative, even though it still makes sense to strive for completeness, using all the resources that may be available to us.

In fact, you had heard that in looking into the possible connections between being and thinking—between what is and the processes for knowing about what is, for being able to say "I know X"—Schleiermacher had come to the view that metaphysics and logic are wholly interdependent and inseparable. Here "metaphysics," as ontology, is supposed to give a general account of being, or at least of how to talk reasonably about being. In another aspect, metaphysics is to consider the basic principles and presuppositions underlying the processes called "knowing." "Logic," in this case, comprises both general rules for forming concepts and judgments and proper ways of understanding their nature and their relations to each other. Yet, logic, perhaps surprisingly, excludes what may be concluded in using demonstrative logic, which has its own technical rules but in which a conclusion may contain only what is already given in the premises. That is, you had been told—it turns out correctly—that for Schleiermacher being and thinking that aims at knowing are supposed to correspond exactly, in that sense to be "identical," thus both ideally and actually to be inseparable. The problem then is how to understand this fundamental relation, which informs and qualifies almost every aspect of our lives, given the uncertainty that is bound up in our efforts to know anything.

In the period in which you actually live, as in Schleiermacher's time, often the forced alternatives on these matters are to take a position somewhere near one of two extremes: to be a thoroughgoing skeptic and make your way the best you can or to form a system that purports to account with certainty for everything once and for all, or nearly so. Today, for almost anyone whose mind is free to think, the quest for certainty is deemed to be virtually dead. So, if you are one of those who take this position, is some near approach to the skeptical extreme the only option you have? Schleiermacher provides a middle way. In laying down this path in the notes he has left behind, he presents perspectives and arguments sufficient, in most instances, for you to follow it in your own thinking.

In one respect you are fortunate that the lectures are not fleshed out for you, because you are thus drawn to think out the matter for yourself. Later you will be able to test out your thinking in examining a much larger body of notes and transcripts in translation (Edwin Mellen Press), which offers Schleiermacher's dialectic from 1811 to 1833, when he began to write an introduction to a book on the subject that was never completed. What I am confident you would find, if you were to do this or to have gained sufficient competency in German to examine the texts independently of any English edition, is a marked consistency of his major proposals and arguments from beginning to end but with some valuable tightening, further insight, elaboration, and additional application as the years go by.

Now, whether you place yourself in 1811 or in the present, you do have the benefit of what I am adding here by way of supplement as editor and by way of interpretation as a reader who is relatively well-informed. I am able gratefully to indicate that much of the formal editorial apparatus has already been supplied by Andreas Arndt, a recent editor of the German text (1986). It has seemed to me that without editorial aids readers of today are likely to find the steady march of abstract substantives in this extremely concise text too difficult to follow with any surety. Although the text itself is quite lucid, it is not meant to lay things out as a lecture would. Moreover, even full lectures such as those provided by Rudolf

Odebrecht (1942) from the 1822 lectures are only one step down the abstraction ladder, as it were, so that an accurate reader even of these must proceed very carefully. Schleiermacher was not much of a one to use concrete references. Like many other philosophical authors, he wants his readers to discover illustrations and to entertain possible applications for themselves. The main purpose, for him, is to set forth the proper ideas and arguments.

The General Meaning and Structure
of Schleiermacher's "Dialectic"

Given this approach to the reading of these very concise notes, the general meaning and structure of the work will reveal itself as you proceed. All through the years, it consisted of two main parts. The "transcendental" part, without conveying any specific empirical information or construction of knowledge, which are tasks for the sciences, lays out the general presuppositions concerning any thinking that can lead to such knowing and its organization for theoretical and practical purposes. The "formal," or "technical," part sets forth general principles for the discovery and formation of methods both for scientific work and for further philosophical work. The actual procedures that are appropriate for any given subject area, problem set, or field of inquiry are to be grounded in these general methodological considerations plus what can be contributed especially by mathematics, the more refined aspects of logic, hermeneutics (as the art of interpretation) and criticism. All these other contributions, insofar as they are to aid in the process of knowing, are likewise grounded in dialectic.

Now, the concept "dialectic" has its own history, as Schleiermacher briefly indicates in the first three lectures. He himself chooses mostly to refer back to the Greeks, especially Plato, at a time when "science" was not so radically separated from philosophy as it has gradually come to be since the fifteenth century. At least in ways just suggested, the natural and human sciences do have tasks of their own for Schleiermacher. Yet, in the critical examination and construction of presuppositions underlying each and every science, in the formation of appropriate methods and procedures, in linking theories and findings across fields, in considering social situations that bear descriptively and normatively on scientific activity and in thinking out practical implications and applications of that activity philosophy can play a crucial role. At the same time, it is likely that science will suffer as to its integrity or its adequacy or its pertinence to human life to the extent that such contributions of a philosophical nature are lacking. These are all beliefs that underlie Schleiermacher's project of dialectic.

These important relations between philosophy and science, however, are scarcely identified in any conscious way in much science today—or, often, in much of the way philosophy is done. Implicitly, they do tend to be present, if not generally in a very deliberate fashion. The overall impression is thus one of helter-skelter activity, the left hand not knowing what the right hand doeth and vice versa.

Unfortunately, if these ties were more deliberate and well-organized, this would be no guarantee of ultimate success in every respect. Still, it is easy to see that gaining greater clarity as to both intellectual and moral issues involved in what we are doing at each hand, as of their likely consequences, could help contemporary thinkers face more effectively the large set of global crises in which all these issues are implicated in some way.

Certainly some thinkers today do go back to the early Greek philosophers and their successors over 2,500 years to look at puzzles and problems and quandaries to be found in their thought and for our own present purposes, just as Schleiermacher did. Or they try to think them through largely without such historical resources, something very difficult to do. The puzzles eventually become familiar and can be fully solved. In contrast, the problems are often virtually intractable, and they may contain, for many, inherently contestable contrasts. This is so not least because different thinkers are likely to bring to the definition of these problems, as to processes aimed at their resolution, presuppositions of value and belief that cannot be readily adjudicated now, if they ever can be. Finally, the quandaries, at least for very long periods of time, turn out to be totally resistant to final settlement. This is so because they seem to be caught within some very basic, troublesome condition inherent in human existence itself.

Here Schleiermacher is reflecting such repeated findings of experience, which appear even at the highest levels of knowledge and reflection. He is saying that we move up the ladder to such resolution as we can obtain toward a point, one not yet reached in any respect, at which union, conceived as a complete and final attainment of identity among contrasts, may be found in what is "absolute." The evidence for such a final, though unreached end, he argues, lies in the fruitfulness for detailed observation and combination that is demonstrated at each successive level upward. He then infers that there must be one ideal-real being, to be presupposed as present even at the lowest level from which human consciousness climbs, and one world that in its own way, as the totality of all our aggregated knowings and only as such, somehow corresponds to that one being. This one being, as united and all-encompassing, is not conceived as existing in the way that any identifiable singular being in the world would exist. In that sense it is not a being, it is not singular or distinctive. Rather, this being exists and can be felt or presupposed in thinking as the source and endpoint of all other being, as the "absolute." At the start and at the finish, then, being and thinking are taken to be one with each other.

Unlike Schleiermacher, the now "classical" American pragmatists (Peirce, James and Dewey chief among them) did not move to the avowedly religious point of a solid beginning, end and substratum to the whole process of thinking that has the aim of knowing. However, they did concern themselves with the question of how to conceive "being" in circumstances wherein the age-old quest for certainty seemed irretrievable in any area of human life, including religion, science and philosophy. Moreover, short of articulating exactly what "being" is at any point—which Schleiermacher also found no grounds to do except on a provisional basis, and even then not in any real, concrete terms with dialectic itself—almost everything within the processes of this type of thinking is very close to, frequently identical with, what the pragmatists were proposing.

It is an historical anomaly that, at the very time many "postmodern" thinkers are identifying their typically much looser approaches to knowing and science with pragmatic thought, demands for better organized, more fully articulated, appropriately exact, firmly cross-disciplinary thinking are also growing. Schleiermacher and his pragmatic successors would appear to be much closer to meeting these latter demands. They are so precisely in the methods by which they explore ways to discover, critique, alter and revise claims to know in a planful manner that weighs consequences as they can be imagined as well as when they appear. Among them, as in Schleiermacher, there is an immense trust that such processes will yield progressively greater apprehensions of "what is" (being), even as "what is" is changing—much of the results having some reliable surety, it may reasonably be hoped, but never the certainties relied on in the past. Likewise, whatever surety arises with respect to knowing the religious forms and content of human life must come, and must make its varied contributions, in the same way. It is no accident, I think, that this great dialectician, Schleiermacher, was also the first great modern religious thinker. He always took the broader view, was always looking for interconnectedness and cohesion among human enterprises overall, was continually plumbing the depths and potential heights of attainment in human development. All these features reside in dialectic and in everything that it points to in that part of life that encompasses philosophy and science. One would have to treat and appraise other sorts of thinking elsewhere, always being critically watchful of what is contained in any claims to "know" in other domains.

What does "Identity" Mean?

I have indicated various relations of "identity" in Schleiermacher's discourse on dialectic, most notably that between thinking and being. This word "identity" is, in fact, frequently used in this discourse and is a potential source of puzzlement. Because it had been a key concept in the metaphysical writings of other philosophers at that time, its appearance in Schleiermacher's discourse has occasioned a rather confusing literature on the subject. Here Schleiermacher does not take pains to clarify what he means, though several meanings can be ferreted out of his text.

(1) "Identity" is never used for a pure coinciding or a mere congruence of two or more things (cf. the 8th lecture, Twesten).

(2) "Identity" can be a strict equivalence, as in mathematics, but is never used that way as between items in actual experience. In other words, except in instances that are clearly mathematical, the identitative sense of the copula ("is"), meaning "exactly the same as, in every respect, thus totally equivalent," is not used; and "is" ordinarily means "exists," "exists as," or "consists of," or "has X as predicate(s)." There may be instances in which "is" refers to one of the sorts of identity to be outlined below, but the tendency would be to add qualifiers that indicate which meaning is intended. For example, an implicit or explicit qualifier might be "speaking only formally" (but not materially) or "for all intents and purposes" (but not exactly) "are the same." Likewise, to say that a given set of things or categories are "one" or "at one" with each other, as is occasionally seen in Schleiermacher's practice, does not necessarily mean that they are "identical" in any of the meanings indicated here.

(3) Ordinarily, "identity" is a technical term that refers either to that which constitutes (is the source of) two quite distinguishable yet mutually implying or presupposing categories or to the interpermeating of two domains such that each is wholly inseparable from the other and inconceivable apart from the other (cf. the 10th lecture, Twesten). Accordingly, in some instances a "sphere of identity" may exist, in which each of two contrasting aspects of thinking serve toward the capacity of the other to discover—for example, the two "moments" that make up the process of deduction (cf. the 43d lecture).

(4) In another technical usage, "identity" points to something's being exhaustively identifiable in the knowing of all persons or subjects (cf. the 9th lecture). Thus, in the ideal sense each specific instance of knowing is identical in all who possess that knowing.

(5) In specific, highly theoretical contexts, "identity" is used here to refer (a) to a dissolution of judgment at the supreme level of thinking, with the result that the two main features of thinking, concept and judgment, once distinguished from

each other, are no longer distinguishable (cf. the 10th–11th lectures), hence are "identical"; (b) to a kind of judgment that consists of two total opposites, namely being and nonbeing, and in which being is the subject of the sentence and nonbeing is the object, and they are thus taken to be "identical"; (c) to the condition of a supreme entity, of which nothing distinct (or determinate) can be predicated (cf. the 11th lecture, Twesten); (d) to that completion or purity that can be accomplished only when an asymptote is supplemented by the idea of the absolute (cf. the 33d lecture). In all such cases, a dissolution of judgment seems to be involved, because the material conditions necessary for making judgments can no longer be posited as present, yet matters that were once discerned to belong together are indistinguishable.

(6) Partly, but still significantly, "identity" may refer not so directly to relations between two or more contrasting concepts or entities as to the relatively steady, constant self-sameness of a single one over time, though not necessarily in every identifiable respect. For example, ultimately "knowing" is depicted as that thinking which is "identical in all," and is thus to be called "reason," despite what may be "different" or "distinctive" in particular persons or instances and once these singular characteristics have been extracted (cf. the 39th lecture). By implication, a person can and will have an identity, quite distinctively so, as in current widespread usage, and that identity can be sought and developed.

Alas, this is all very technical, but it is meant to serve a greater exactness in the reading.

Reason and Irrationality, Truth and Error

Not much needs saying under this heading just now. I simply want to alert the reader to the very high status that Schleiermacher gives to "reason" and to how he conceives of truth and error. The term "reason" refers to what is known in common, and ideally in the most fully accomplished way, by all thinkers who have striven to know. Sometimes in Schleiermacher's writings, "reason" seems almost to bear the characteristics of a great being, in keeping with an Enlightenment tradition represented especially by Immanuel Kant. This usage is to be understood as a recognition of the commonality among all persons who truly know. That is, none will have achieved this knowing strictly on one's own; many will have contributed significantly; all are in the end joint possessors of knowledge and are at the same time possessed by reason, as it were.

For Schleiermacher, truth, under the real (empirically noticeable) conditions of all knowing, is never absolute in any sense; it is always mixed with some error. The reverse is also true, as Schleiermacher argues. The task of the would-be knower is to try to sort out the more nearly truthful—for this is always in process of development—from error, honoring the difficulties that bearers may have encountered along the way. In its most generally applicable sense, the word "irrational," which Schleiermacher rarely uses, would refer to the condition of being far off the mark of truth, error-filled. In another closely related sense, it would mean not using the means of reason or not holding to the ideals of reason. Finally, this word could also mean allowing oneself to be controlled by whatever gets in the way of being reasonable in one's thinking, notably by ignorance or by undue passion.

Because of the highly important status that Schleiermacher affords to feeling, he never strictly identifies being "irrational" with "having feelings" or "being emotional," as is often done by others; nor does he identify "feeling" as another, sometimes perhaps better way of knowing. Although in today's terms perhaps what he means by "feeling" can be fruitfully thought of as a specific kind of knowing, this is not, in my view, supportable in terms of Schleiermacher's own concept of knowing. As will be seen here, as throughout his writings, the pair "feeling" and "perception," differently defined at several levels of mentation, are nonetheless always at least potentially significant components of any effective thinking, of any knowing whatsoever, as of any moral action. For Schleiermacher, they are inextricable parts of who human beings are. Certainly they can be ignored or underplayed, or left underdeveloped. All three actions are likely to be involved in attempts totally to separate the religious domain, which at its deepest sources is itself a matter of "feeling" and "perception," from any other domain of human life.

Religion, Dialectic, and the Other Domains of Life

In the early editions of *On Religion* (1799, 1806), Schleiermacher already viewed religion not only in terms of a higher feeling and perception, by which his approach is popularly distinguished, but also as by its very nature socially constructed, taking communal, institutional form, and capable of development in itself and in persons. By its very nature, it was therefore seen to be distinctively connected with all the other domains of human life. Later he showed that it is variously a task of the philosophy of religion, theology and ethics (the human sciences), not of dialectic, to show this interconnectedness in detail. Nevertheless, the grounds for such a richly constructed approach are briefly set forth in his 1811 presentation of dialectic, along with strict limitations as to the treatment of religion within the bounds of philosophy.

Schleiermacher offers no extended account of how the religious domain and 'God' relate to the rest of what is explicated in the 1811 notes. Thus, one must draw upon what he does say there and by that time in order to reconstruct how far he had advanced toward what he more fully developed in later notes and lectures. This reconstruction can still be quite substantial, as will now be shown.

Already in his 1789 essay *On the Highest Good* and at a time when his primary interest in ethics was to find in reason the ground for a universal morality, Schleiermacher opposed Kant's conceiving 'God' as a postulate of morality, holding this to be both unnecessary, as contravening Kant's own critical principles in *The Critique of Pure Reason* (1881) and as based on "the natural illusion of speculative reason" (22f.).[1] Through a series of breakthroughs related in his 1800 *Soliloquies*, Schleiermacher also parted from the Leibnizian-Wolffian rationalist tradition of metaphysics,[2] long prominent in the University at Halle where he was then studying. Instead, he sought to grasp the moral domain without recourse to their invasive postulates of God and immortality. Within a few years he was proposing to view historical phenomena as continually in process, as in development, and as empirically distinctive yet not to be separated from changing, advancing visions of the whole. Both realism and idealism were then rejected in favor of a more dynamic though still comprehensive view of reality. This series of breakthroughs experienced in the 1790s, most of them before his famous involvement in the creation of early German Romanticism after he moved to Berlin in 1796, was permanent in its effect, though Schleiermacher continued to apply interests that had arisen in earlier traditions, both rationalist and empirical, in radically revised form.

Schleiermacher's 1790–1792 essay *On Freedom* is a living testimony to his severance from both Kant and the Leibnizian-Wolffians in this respect. There he went only so far beyond the limits placed on concepts by critical reason as to conceive the deity in this context as "the undetermined cause of all determined things" (129). In addition, but against both fatalistic and mystical views, he was willing to hold the position that God regulates actions in such a way that "they mesh in the determinate order of the material world and its accidental changes, and in such a way that, among themselves, they constitute a whole foreknown by the Supreme Being" (106). The subject who is free, however, does not simply happen upon a given action ordained by God and is not inalterably determined to that action. Both of these rejected views wrongly presuppose an influence from outside that is "cut off from the interconnectedness of the subject's states" (109).

---

1. See my translation of a passage in the 1800 *Soliloquies* referring to this period in Victor Froese's edition of *On the Highest Good* (Lewiston, N.Y.: Edwin Mellen Press, 1995) and my reference to this and to the major "breakthrough" in 1794 that led him away from a universalist approach in the edition by Edwina Lawler and me of the 1792–1793 essay *On What Gives Value to Life* (same publisher, 1995), p. xvii.

2. Cf. Albert L. Blackwell's edition of *On Freedom* (same publisher, 1992), p. x, where he notes agreement with Günter Meckenstock on this point. My translation of the *Soliloquies* is forthcoming in the same Schleiermacher: Studies and Translations series.

This subject, as a "spiritual being," possesses a disposition freely to act within a general interconnectedness of nature on which one is dependent, in response to obligation placed on oneself by the moral law and held accountable for one's acts of choice. The lawgiving wisdom of God, if it is to be affirmed in the moral domain, consists in providing at once for just such a determinism and just such a freedom.

In the 1792–1793 essay *On What Gives Value to Life* Schleiermacher did assert that fate, in the general sense of "the entire disposition of nature," is indeed "just" (78), but, if the term is to be used at all, fate is also "generous," "gracious" (78, 83). This is true not in the sense of the deity's distributing happiness in various amounts, however, but in the sense, grasped by a higher "moral feeling," that there is much that can give value to life that transcends mere happiness and has "a highest purpose" as its end. The Supreme Being (36) that is taken to be "governing the world," the "rational, ordering being at the apex of things," provides room for a person's free development toward that end (79).

Thus far, Schleiermacher's aim was almost entirely critical and negative. That is, he emphasized what one could not reasonably say and set limits on what could reasonably be said. Still, there are also clear signs of the young theological student's faith (he was ordained in 1794), of his sense for God. The 1799 discourses *On Religion*[3] displayed a full-fledged view of religion and God, one both critical and substantive. By then he was also opposing the "purely speculative idealist" (45)—notably Fichte, though not by name—and was searching out "the highest reaches of the Kingdom of God" (46). In this work he was carving out a specific domain for religion, defined not by speculative reason or morality but by the sheer feeling and perceptiveness at "the innermost depths" (51) that he designated by the term "piety." In this context, then, he wished to affirm a communion in faith with "the living God" (51). At this time, the critical limits placed on discourse about God that he later articulated in the successive notes and lectures on dialectic are also clearly indicated in this lengthy set of essays, as were the solid boundaries between religion and reason, religion and morality. Here too, he points out the mediating function of genuine religious consciousness between these other two domains.

Further, we are stirred to sense or know God, he contends, only in and through the world (the *universum*). Thus, 'God' and 'world', though not identical, are correlates; God is affirmed to be in first place, the biblical "Highest," and transcendent over the world, but except in feeling we cannot relate to God as having these characteristics, and we cannot know God except

---

3. The forthcoming revision of my 1969 translation of *On Religion*, to appear in the above-mentioned series, retains the same pagination of the main 1821 text, with additions in footnotes and at the end indicating revisions and all differences in 1799 and 1806 editions.

under the condition of the world we have, including our own nature. Nor does religion itself require having a prior conception of God, though within a given religious community it may be unthinkable to be religious without the accompaniment of some conception of God. Indeed, as a religious person who has a consciousness of God the domains of morality and reason may well come to be integrally related in one's life, as was manifestly the case for Schleiermacher himself. Morality and reason do not as such determine the nature of one's inner religious experience (later: immediate religious self-consciousness), however; the direction rather goes the other way.

Now, this general approach Schleiermacher further developed and explicated over the three and a half remaining decades of his life, but he never departed from it, not even in his most strictly philosophical works.

The University of Berlin, where Schleiermacher was a professor of theology but regularly taught courses in philosophy throughout his career there, was opened in 1810. Schleiermacher reached his forty-third birthday on November 21, 1811. In his note preparatory to the 23d lecture on dialectic in 1811, he avers that "we have the absolute as reason," but we are not the absolute and do not have its concept, nor do we have it from the site of organic function (ordinary perception); rather, we have it "only as the formal element common to all acts of cognition." "Thus," he continues: "We are involved in forming a vital perspective on the deity to the extent that we work on the completion of the real sciences" (see also the 18th lecture)—not, however, by adding details to an aggregate but by "systematic treatment" that strives for the totality of all this. So: "Except to assert that the deity as transcendent being is the principle of all being and as transcendent idea is the formal principle of all knowing, nothing more is to be said of it in the domain of knowing. All else is simply bombast or an admixing of the religious, which is out of bounds here and can actually have only a corruptive effect if placed within the bounds." In separate aphorisms preparatory to the 1811 lectures[4] Schleiermacher states: "The inconceivability of God is demonstrable. No concept of God can correspond to the absolute concept." "God is not to be thought of other than as in and under a distinct

---

4. See Friedrich Daniel Ernst Schleiermacher, *Dialektik* (1811), hg.v. Andreas Arndt (Hamburg: Felix Meiner, 1986), lxxxiv, 115 p.; here the citation is at page 74, aphorisms 113 and 119 from Bruno Weiss's Beilage G (in his three-part essay on Schleiermacher's dialectic, 1878–1800). Although the text used for the present translation is that of Ludwig Jonas, *Dialektik*, Bd 4:2 in Schleiermacher's *Sämmtliche Werke* (Berlin: G. Reimer, 1839), xviii, 609 p., especially of Beilag A (313–361), Arndt's virtually unchanged text adds important apparatus also occasionally referred to here. This is one example. Also referred to below is his edition of Schleiermacher's *Dialektik* (1814/15) and *Einleitung zur Dialektik* (1833) (same publisher, 1988), xxxiv, 177 p. Here the main text is also virtually unchanged. It is made the basis both in Jonas's edition and in that of all the dialectic texts being prepared for the Edwin Mellen Press series by Joseph Eckenrode and myself.

perception, just as in the religious domain too God is not to be felt other than in this way."

Accordingly, in the first edition of his *Brief Outline of Theology as a Field of Study* (also in 1811),[5] §1, Schleiermacher refers to Christian theology as "positive." That is, its parts "join into a cohesive whole only through their common relation to a particular religion." (In 1830 he there refers to "a particular mode of faith, that is, a particular way of being conscious of God," and he further explains, in a way wholly consistent with the 1811 notes on dialectic, that in theological science, thus oriented, the 'God' of speculative science—of rationalists and so-called natural theology—is not a part of genuine theology.)

In keeping with these views, Schleiermacher states the following in his notes for the 1811 course on dialectic, lecture 17: "What is absolute is not to be thought of as a singular thing that is exhausted only in an infinity of judgments; nor is it to be thought of as a concept caught in the identity between a lower and higher concept. Its concept also cannot lie outside what is absolute itself. We can have what is absolute only granted the inadequacy of any image of deity we have in the identity of our being and our concept. There is no such thing as an isolated perception of deity. Rather, we perceive the deity only in and with the collective system of perception. The deity is just as surely incomprehensible as the knowledge of it is the basis of all knowledge. Exactly the same is true also on the side of feeling." This concise statement directly refers, without alteration, to positions for which he had argued in *On Religion*, both in the original 1799 edition and in the revised edition of 1806. The only difference lies in the mode of discourse.

Along the same line, in notes for the second lecture he affirms: "No one can have the idea of God without knowing how this supreme entity can be impressed within some particular, how this supreme entity would relate to the world." Moving in the other direction, in notes for the 15th lecture he claims: "'God' is no postulate that would have to be given so as actually to effectuate real knowing"—that is, it cannot be a postulate of either pure or practical reason (contra Kant). The notes for lectures 24–25 then offer a fairly lengthy comparison of his view of deity with other views, all strictly within the context of thinking as knowing. There he indicates his assumption that "the idea of deity is present in everything" within that context and that God is thus "not to be separated from the world." This view he pits against "spiritualism" (including absolute idealism), "materialism" (even of a theistic kind), and any view that posits the world as eternal without God or that posits God as happening to have thoughts about the world, which would then simply become temporal through

5. See the revision of my 1966 edition of Schleiermacher's *Brief Outline of Theology as a Field of Study* (Lewiston, N.Y.: Edwin Mellen Press, 1990), xv, 230 p.

God. Even here, however, he does not identify God merely with the transcendental aspect to which dialectical reasoning refers, for the formal, technical
aspect is regarded as forming "a unity" with that first aspect. In this and other
ways, he also opposes any suggestion of mere subjectivism, for reason is a
common achievement among all thinking minds and must coherently correspond
with being. It is only more clearly worked out in later years that, in this limited
formal respect, 'God' is the transcendental ground of all thinking that aims at
knowing. There was no change of perspective either in this respect or in the
view that to say anything more of God is to enter into the religious domain and to
be ensconsed in conditions of the "real" world—the finite, organic, perceptible
world—and in the contrasts that inevitably accompany thinking as knowing.

Moreover, in the 1814/1815 notes on dialectic only three years later,
Schleiermacher also remains consistent with his thinking both earlier and later in
saying: "We have knowledge concerning the being of God only in us and in
things but not at all concerning a being of God outside the world or in itself"
(§216). The idea of deity as absolute being is true only "insofar as deity is the
vital foundation of all process" (§126). "As deity is the locus of all vital powers,
so reason is the locus of all true concepts" (§176.3). Even though one can validly
speak of "the indwelling being of God as the principle of all knowing," this is
true only with respect to knowing oriented to the real world (§44). The
differentiation of the two is clearcut. The differentiation of God from nature is
also clearcut (cf. §§183–184 and §§187–188). Thus, a natural theology "can
never be validated as an expression of religious consciousness" (§184.2). God
and world are correlates but are not identical (§§219–229); nor do concepts of
fate and providence correspond to the deity here (§202).

All these arguments and positions form a consistent whole, based on
reflections that were building up in earlier years, from his students days on.
Aspects of this now mature position reached by 1811, and only further refined
and explicated in later years, may well be identified with inquiries and positions
that scholars variously affix to propadeutic, foundational or philosophical
theology. They certainly do serve to set parameters for both inquiry about
religion and genuine "positive" theology, and in the process they do reject
numerous claims, clearing away much that Schleiermacher took to be mere
deadwood, whatever would obfuscate vital religion and the living God. Yet, they
do not express religious consciousness, they have no "positive" function. In his
thinking on dialectic over the next two decades, Schleiermacher steadily held to
this same course, investigating the grounds for correlated metaphysical/logical
inquiry in philosophy and thereby the grounds for all thinking that aims at
genuine knowing. Beyond all knowing, though in real terms interwoven with
knowing as a key aspect of life, lies the heart of religion, lies faith. This can

certainly be studied and to an extent represented, but it can never be wholly grasped by either concepts or judgments. Insofar as it is in touch with its ultimate object through a higher feeling and perception, it is transcendent over all else and stands profoundly to affect all else.

In this way, the sparse presuppositions set forth here, in opposition to overly grand, moribund alternatives, open out toward surprisingly broad, richly variegated vistas within the domain of religion. It is only fitting that in his philosophical role the founder of the modern study of religion should provide this.

INTRODUCTION:
THE GENERAL PART

Lecture 1
(Monday, April 22, 1811)

Over the system of coordinated sciences there must be certain principles they share, an architectonic for these principles.[6] However much one is to expect

---

6. Ed. note: The lectures were offered on Monday through Wednesday from 5:00 to 6:00 p.m. Since Schleiermacher's preparatory notes for lecture hours 1–11 (beginning Monday, April 22, 1811) are not extant, it is of great value to have August Twesten's highly creditable summary notes and elaborations from these hours. See also Ludwig Jonas's synopses from a set of lecture notes no longer available in SW III.4:2 (1839) and in Andreas Arndt's edition (1986), 83–95. Twesten's notes comprise the main text for these lecture hours. His elaborations are given in notes here. The first set of Twesten's notes (Arndt, 84–85) provide a helpful introductory overview covering roughly the first six lectures, as follows.

"1. The science of the supreme principles of knowing divorced from the real sciences or set over against them is unsatisfactory and mortifying of the human mind. By the same token, without that science no scientific procedure can be formulated.

"2. The supreme principles of knowing and of scientific construction are at one with each other; transcendental philosophy and formal philosophy are not to be divorced from each other. Nevertheless, in their presentation reference can be made, respectively, to scientific construction (the art of doing philosophy) and to the supreme and most general knowing.

"3. In accordance with Plato's usage, we term the science of supreme principles "dialectic," which is thus positioned over ethics and physics.

"4. Dialectic is the organon of all the sciences, and by means of it every bit of information that comes up can be assigned its place within the entire compass of science. However, it does not produce information and is thus of itself empty in that respect.

"5. There is no opposition between a higher (rational) and a lower (empirical) knowing. All knowing becomes knowing through entry of the principles of knowing, hence there is no instance of knowing to which dialectic would not know how to assign its place, for everything belongs within the system of knowing.

"6. Skepticism does not touch dialectic. The reasons are these: (a) Either it asserts that no information can be subsumed under the idea of knowing, and then it gives recognition to the laws of combination and with them the principles of dialectic. (b) Or it refers to the contrastive nature of the assertions of reason, which is supposed to arrange for some unity,

unity in all these principles, unity is just as little available nonetheless, and the diversity among these principles extends its influence over all the other sciences.

To do philosophy concerning these first principles without regard for what is real seems to be something unsatisfactory and for science dangerous, especially if that practice quite likely has as a result some sort of opposition between speculation and real knowing.[7]

---

and intends therefrom to show the impossibility of knowing whether something is an instance of knowing; and then it gives recognition to a law of unity, and thus whatever truth lies in its assertions lies outside the domain of dialectic. (c) Since skepticism does not declare the idea of knowing to be inconceivable, it gives recognition to that idea, and indeed as having a living presence, as something that effects a striving to know, for otherwise it would have no object to fight over.

"7. If all knowing becomes an instance of knowing only through the entry of the principle of knowing, how can there be an instance of knowing in anyone before one's possession of dialectic, since such an instance of knowing does indisputably exist?

"As was said, there is not twofold nature of knowing, for the unity of consciousness would be annulled by such a twofold nature. It is also evident that there is no difference in knowing in the way anyone discovers it in oneself before and after one's possession of dialectic. However, one can possess the principles of knowing in a twofold way, unconsciously, as sheer agency, in the form of activity and taken up into consciousness. In the first, unconscious form these principles compose everything that comes to be present in us in the form of knowing; in the second, conscious form they comprise the task of taking up the knowing of the first kind by means of them in the form of science, without the two forms either of knowing or of consciousness thereby being particularly different. The contrast is always rather a relative one.

"8. How can one come to these supreme principles other than by already being acquainted with them?

"If one divorces the transcendental and formal principles from each other, this is no different from presupposing the correctness of but one of these, in which case it is, however, not possible to gain certitude that one is not in error.

"If one takes the transcendental and the formal to be one, this oneness must be contained in the form of every given instance of knowing (even of what is erroneous, for to find what is absolute we must abstract from what is accidental, which taken by itself can perhaps be amiss). The assumption that something absolute is contained in all particular instances of knowing is, of course, not of equal worth compared with what issues therefrom; thus, to that extent one must also give recognition to belief's being prior to knowing. However, the other way around, the active element in all our convictions is still arranged by the principles of knowing.

"9. As a force, the supreme knowing is accordingly the principle from which every real knowing arises, even if the latter is incomplete. As something consciously held, it is the principle from which science regarding what is real arises. We search for this supreme knowing, however, in that we proceed from some particular recognized to be an instance of knowing."

Ed. note: Schleiermacher starts off somewhat differently in other years—e.g. compare the first nine lectures, from Oct. 24 on, in 1814 (##1–85) and the five elucidated introductory propositions in 1833—both included in an Andreas Arndt edition (1988). Yet, the point of view and arrangement of concepts remains nearly the same.

7. *Reales Wissen*. Ed. note: Throughout *Wissen* is translated "knowing," which here refers to a process aimed at producing "knowledge" (*Erkenntnis*), or, lacking that, at least "information" (*Kenntnisse*). The corresponding verbs "to know" are *kennen* (sometimes

While some people are of the opinion that all scientific culture must begin with speculation, others want to place speculation at its end, where it is less in a position to hinder the working of that culture in human life. Only through acquaintance with the first principles is there an escape from the empirical and the beaten path, on the one hand, and from arbitrariness, on the other. Now, in recent times much arbitrariness does indeed seem to have arisen from speculation; this, however, has not been its fault but the fault of its being isolated—the actual error to be warned against.

The scientific spirit overall and talent for first principles are not disparate. Thus, in itself speculative talent in no way stands in opposition to talent regarding what is real. Only its being isolated bears a destructive effect. Moreover, the two are always to be practiced only cooperatively.[8]

Lecture 2

The term "dialectic" is chosen in part because use of another term[9] could easily have inspired the opinion that this presentation belongs within the circle of a certain school that would have selected this other term, and in part to designate what is distinctive about this presentation. That is to say, by "dialectic" we mean the principles of the art of doing philosophy.[10]

---

meaning just "to be acquainted with") and *erkennen* (which with *anerkennen* sometimes means "to recognize"). "Cognition" translates the much rarer *Erkennen* (a noun). On "real knowing," see the commentary just below.

8. Ed. commentary: Implied here, then, is (a) the view that insofar as philosophy critiques and provides the first principles underlying each and all of the sciences, it takes part in science and (b) the view that insofar as this activity continually draws upon what is real, thus is accessible to empirical investigation, but practices talents for speculative and empirical inquiry "cooperatively," not isolating them from each other, it is itself a part of the sciences and in that sense is scientific, a science in its own right. In his second 1814 lecture Schleiermacher indicates that previously philosophy had not gained the status of being a science, even though as he conceives it philosophy is "the supreme science." He adds that as the sciences become more mature "all science bears the intention of being art and all art of being science, and indeed the moreso the higher level each has reached on its side." In the next hour in 1811, Schleiermacher chooses to emphasize the character of this activity, which he calls "dialectic," as an "art" (*Kunst*—essentially a craft but containing elements that make it more creative than is true of simply reproductive crafts), one that finds and contains the principles for doing philosophy. He does this, however, with the understanding that "some scientific view or other is determined by it" (*bestimmt*—that is, is defined, takes distinct form through its use).

9. Ed. note: Johann Gottlieb Fichte (1762–1814), particularly in reference to his *Wissenschaftslehre* (1794). In 1811 Fichte was lecturing on "theory of science," the other term, at the same hours as Schleiermacher but in a smaller chamber.

10. Ed. note: The announcement of this 1811 course stated: "*Dialecticen s. artis philosophandi principiorum summam*" (dialectic, that is, the entire compass of principles for the art of doing philosophy). "Doing philosophy" translates *zu philosophiren*, since the transliteration "philosophizing" has often borne a negative connotation parallel to

People attribute the term "doing philosophy" both to direct investigations concerning the principles of knowing and to fragmentary investigations concerning individual subjects. In both instances people are seeking to effect some knowledge, of a sort that refers to the principles of knowing, for even the individual subjects, consideration of which is termed "doing philosophy," must be such that some scientific view or other is determined by them. Thus, all doing of philosophy is a legitimate construction[11] of some knowledge, which knowledge is ever of the sort that some science, whether individual or conceived in general terms, is determined by it.

To do philosophy is to bring about some knowledge, united with the clear consciousness of its being brought about. Thus, it falls within the category of art, and its product is therefore also a work of art, for a work of art is something individual within which what is general is directly presented and something infinite is contained. Within every individual thing that arises upon the path of doing philosophy there lies at the same time what is supremely general,[12] the principle according to which it came into being; however, a subjective element is always present in every individual thing that arises upon some other path.

In the case of every other art a medium appears between what is to be presented and the presentation, disturbing its purity. Such a medium is not present here. On this account, and because the art of doing philosophy subsumes the idea of all other arts under itself, it is, as the production of knowledge, the highest art.

Yet, the question arises: Are the principles of this art of cognition and the principles of knowing the same?

To be sure, there is a contrast between science and art, but one that seems increasingly to lessen the higher one rises.

"theologizing." In his first 1814 lecture Schleiermacher defines *philosophiren* "in the strict sense as doing philosophy (*die Philosophie...machen*)—that is, producing the internal interconnectedness of all knowing."

11. *Konstruiren.* Ed. note: In both English and the corresponding German usage "construe" and "construct" refer to the same Latin word *construere*, hence the root meaning of "construe" as to place a construction on, as in interpreting or translating sentences. Schleiermacher's usage of the verb throughout these lectures is exactly parallel to that of the noun *Construction*, which he also employs.

12. *Das höchste Allgemeine.* Ed. commentary: As will be seen, Schleiermacher is presupposing a rising scale from the simplest, most particular entities, themselves attached to the lowest possible level of generality, up through an indeterminable number of stages to the highest or supreme level of generality. Hence, the tendency of some to think of what is general as "universal" is very much mistaken as applied to his thought. Schleiermacher carefully reserves the terms *universelles* and *Universum* for universality, and sometimes even *universelles* is simply contrasted to *individuelles*, without any reference to level of generality. With respect to real knowing, knowing that is focused on what is accessibly real, the general and the particular are seen always, inseparably, to bear upon and to qualify each other.

One could say that the principles on which and according to which science is constructed would be something different. However, with the highest principles this contrast disappears. No one, for example, can have the idea of God without knowing how this supreme entity[13] can be impressed within a particular, how this supreme entity would relate to the world. Conjointly with the highest principles of knowing is posited the way in which one perceives what is highest in a particular and produces what is particular from it.[14]

Of course, one will be able to distinguish the actual principle of this construction from strictly technical rules; however, in granting this no further contrast enters in, if the knowledge in question is not to be purely negative in character.

The supreme and most general elements of knowing, therefore, and the principles for doing philosophy themselves are the same. Thus, transcendental philosophy and formal philosophy are, if they are to contain something real, the same. Contrary to Kant, constitutive and regulative principles do not admit of distinction.[15]

Lecture 3

Entirely in accord with this concept is the term "dialectic," which had precisely this meaning among the ancients,[16] for the contrast between real science

---

13. *Dies Höchste*.

14. Ed. commentary: Thus far, much of the literature on Schleiermacher's dialectic concentrates on this idea of God, mostly because of its possible connections to theology. However important the term may be, he uses it quite sparingly, and his aim throughout is to do philosophy and to talk about how to do it, not to do theology.

15. Ed. note: As Arndt points out, Schleiermacher adopts this distinction from Immanuel Kant (1724–1804). See especially Kant's Foreward to the second edition of his *Kritik der reinen Vernunft* (*Critique of Pure Reason*) (1787), where he refers to "all knowledge (*Erkenntnis*) that deals not so much with objects as with our way of knowing objects insofar as this is to be possible a priori" as "transcendental." This, says Kant, is to be distinguished from the merely formal rules for thinking, which do not particularly refer to their objects or to the content of knowledge, that is, from "logic," which is comprised entirely of these formal rules, whether they are a priori or empirical in nature. Note, too, that whereas Kant uses "knowledge" here, Schleiermacher regularly uses *Wissen*, which in its form as a verbal noun refers to a process, one that enables one or more persons to say "I (we) know," "am (are) knowing"—that is, "have or am (are) getting knowledge."

In his Foreword to the second edition of his *Kritik der Urteilskraft* (*Critique of Judgment*) (1793) Kant had affirmed a distinction between constitutive and regulative principles. Schleiermacher rejects this distinction, thus also any distinction between "transcendent" and "transcendental" (see the next hour).

16. Ed. note: Compare Schleiermacher's 1812 account in his history of philosophy lectures, SW III.4.1 (1839), pp. 18, 98–99. There he likewise distinguishes between ethics and physics as together comprising the "real aspect" of the domain of knowledge and refers to dialectic as representing "the general element," which operates negatively, polemically, against

and philosophy did not exist for them. Philosophy encompassed for them ethics, physics and dialectic, the latter of which contained the principles for the other two. For Plato dialectic contained both the rules for constructing science and teachings concerning the real being of what is (*ontos on*) and of the good (*agathon*) to the extent that they had not yet passed at all into the domains of the two remaining disciplines.

The term refers to the art of accomplishing a philosophical construction together with another person. In the Socratic school dialogue took the place of the arbitrary diatribes of the sophists; hence for them the principles for dialogue and for construction of knowledge overall were the same.[17] Thereby the general validity of the principles applying to each was set forth at the same time.

Dialectic was also, at the same time, criticism and contained the criteria by which one could recognize what was science and what was not. This aspect of dialectic is simply a natural outflow of the two parts that are necessarily posited in dialectic.

What have been called metaphysics and logic in modern times were nothing other than these two parts of dialectic in isolation from each other and, on this account, robbed of their proper life; for this reason, no bridge remained extending from metaphysics to physics and ethics, and thereby arose the error that people designate by the term "transcendent." In this separation metaphysics came to be something quite evanescent. On the other side, logic was just as vacuous and inconsequential, and so the result of this separation was the death of philosophy.

Dialectic is thus the identity of the supreme and most general knowing itself and of the principles of scientific construction. In their presentation, however,

---

lower-level reflection; positively, this general element nonetheless retains some "mythological form." To be able to combat sophistical arguments and positions effectively, one needs to be in possession of "the true combinatory art," which Plato called "dialectic," since the ancients "could not divorce thinking and speaking from each other and every dispute was still a lively conversation." In its two aspects, "knowing what can and cannot be connected and knowing how these can be divided or combined," dialectic leads to the unity of contrasts conceived as an absolute unity. "In this fashion not only is Plato's dialectic, on its formal side, then the mirroring of what is real, both physical and ethical, but here the heuristic principle regarding absolute unity or the ideal of deity, which he always simply presupposed in his physical or ethical presentations, also awakens." In this absolute unity or idea, *ontos on* and *agathon* are themselves united (110).

17. Ed. commentary: Although in his later lectures Schleiermacher more often used the term *Streit* (conflict, or dispute) for this exchange of views, this early concept of dialogue was retained, meaning ideally an open-minded, mutually respectful, inquiry-based interplay among thinkers who share the basic aim of coming to know. Moreover, the set of dispositions represented by this concept is everywhere evident in Schleiermacher's own habits of communicating. Recently it has come to be known that in his student days this understanding of relationship in Schleiermacher's thought and practice profoundly influenced Martin Buber, later author of the famous work highlighting dialogue entitled *I and Thou* (Gerda Schmidt, 1995). See note 18 just below.

the one or the other can come to the fore in relative terms, and this must happen in every actual presentation by virtue of the special nature of what is being presented. So, dialectic will appear here especially from the viewpoint of theory concerning philosophical art.[18]

Lecture 4

In this sense dialectic can rightly be called the organon of all science. In relation to the whole of science it is, as it were, what the given center and farthest periphery is to a sphere. By means of it one can assign to each individual proposition its place and can find which organic part of the whole it is; to that extent it is thus, as it were, a supplement to information concerning the whole. Hence, it is based not on a particular talent but only on sensibility of a general scientific kind and makes it possible to appropriate what talent has engendered. Furthermore, only by means of this organon is a genuine knowing possible, to which only an approximation is possible through sheer talent.

Also it is dialectic that conditions communication, the exchange of ideas. Facility for all understanding depends on it. This is so, for one must be able to construct any notion through it, and indeed in such a way that one is in a position to distinguish what is true and what is erroneous in it. No knowing will admit of being exhibited that would not stand in immediate interconnection with this organon, even if it has not yet been assumed into a scientific whole. The interest of dialectic arises because each person strives to join the particular that one has found by means of one's particular talent to what is general; consequently, it is indeed related as something of a general nature to what is individual; however, because one can reproduce what is individual only by means of something general, in itself and divorced from what is particular it is also simply vacuous.

---

18. Ed. note: Jonas's summary in SW III.4:2 (1839), p. 17, from a student transcript, is instructive here. He writes: "Dialectic = the art of exchanging thoughts, the art of sustaining with another an orderly construction of thoughts wherefrom some instance of knowing proceeds. It could seem a marvel that the primary philosophical discipline could take on such a special name. This is easily explained, however, for as people discovered the principles for doing philosophy the freer composition of poetic modes of doing philosophy that had had currency up to that time would be seen as sheer arbitrariness, and the dialogue of the Socratic school arose as a way to be freed from this arbitrariness, and this dialogue form and scientific construction were one and the same thing. Something still more profound lies in this term, without which it certainly would not have had currency so long, namely the commonality (*Gemeinschaftlichkeit*) of thinking and construction, the identity of principles and procedures, in everyone."

Contrary to what is often assumed, there is no antithesis between the highest knowing and common knowing.[19]

Before we get on with our business, we have to take a glance at that skepticism which denies all knowing. Through this denial the skeptic asserts that the idea of knowing is an empty rubric under which nothing could be subsumed. The skeptic must at least acknowledge principles for joining thoughts, hence does not fight against dialectic. Since the skeptic then further claims to have some knowing nevertheless, namely that one knows nothing, the skeptic must on that basis still acquiesce to there being some manifold.[20]

Hence, a less blatant form of skepticism is this: one cannot know whether one knows or not. It shows, accordingly, how to every particular assertion another particular assertion opposes what it has raised. Yet, precisely in that way this form of skepticism already recognizes something similar and thus a supreme law of unity. Thus, if there is some truth in what this skeptic asserts, this must lie in the domain of what is real but not in that wherewith we are concerned. Rather, the truth is that no particular detail can entirely correspond to its idea.

Skepticism also lets the idea of knowing stand, even stand as something vital toward which one strives, for if the skeptic does not acknowledge this idea, such a person has merely to say that it is something that the person has absolutely no ability to imagine. Thus, even from this aspect we remain outside any collision with skepticism.

Lecture 5

In order to secure the relationship of human beings to the world, a number of people affirm an analogue of knowing, be it then called belief or opinion, on which the activity of human beings can be grounded. Such a secondary knowing would have to be something different from what would result from supreme principles. Thus, the consciousness wherein it appears must be an entirely different one, so that a twofold expression of human nature is posited. If one looks at

---

19. Ed. commentary: A major aim in these lectures is to indicate in general terms the interconnectedness of all being and also of all ways of knowing. Partly by means of the concept of a scale comprised of stages (see note 6 above) and partly by other means yet to be discussed, he is thus able to reject any claim of the sort mentioned in this passage. Such a recognition also facilitates exercise of a rather egalitarian sensibility in practical life, e.g. in contrast to one that radically separates an elite class from other classes. In just such brief statements within this set of notes, Schleiermacher is thus able to suggest how attitudes about knowing and science can profoundly affect practical affairs.

20. *Mannigfaltigkeit.* Ed. note: "Manifold" (or multiplicity, manifoldness) ordinarily refers to the varied and numerous sources available in sense-oriented experience. Thus, the skeptic's admission is that there is something complex out there that requires its being dealt with by thinking.

the content of information, this doubled sphere cannot be displayed. If one looks at the potency of consciousness, a distinction would arise between those who are in possession of speculation and those who are not. Even some who, with us, oppose skepticism acknowledge such a distinction. One has to recognize this same split, however, also in the consciousness of those who are supposedly in possession of absolute knowing. In this fashion, therefore, the unity of life is annulled, pure knowing moves only parallel to common knowing, and it is not possible to construct one from the other.[21]

All knowing depends on an original knowing wherewith the laws of all construction of knowing are given at the same time. We proceed on this assumption. It thus seems as though until one would possess this supreme knowing, of necessity one would not be able to know anything else. However, this contradicts the experience not only of individuals but of entire peoples as well. Now, how then can knowing that preceded knowing of what is highest be the same as that which proceeded from that knowing? Two options present themselves here. Either one must recognize a twofold nature of knowing—but by the attainment of absolute knowing no difference whatsoever appears to enter into real knowing, indeed one cannot even say that its scientific form will have emerged from the attainment of supreme knowing, since it arises instead through the greater abundance of materials. Or there must be two ways in which one can possess supreme knowing, and this is the case. How so? Through our search for supreme principles, do we want first to posit ourselves as being in possession of something? We rather presuppose it as existing already and want simply to attain the consciousness of it; it exists in all our knowing but previously in an unconscious way and only under the form of activity; it is indeed something actually at work, but it is not also taken up into consciousness. So, we cannot term the way in which a knowing exists in us, as it evolved at first and as it carries the task with it of taking that knowing up into the form of science by means of supreme principles, as in any specific way different from what is speculative, and so, only a relative contrast exists between the two, since even in what is speculative many an element bears the subordinate form in itself and on

---

21. Ed. note: This discussion is directed especially against a notable position taken by Fichte in his *Die Anweisungen zum seligen Leben, oder auch die Religionslehre* (1806). In a remarkable letter to Wilhelm von Dohna, probably in the summer of 1796, Schleiermacher had reflected an account of opinion, belief and knowing as comprising three successive stages by Kant in the *Kritik der reinen Vernunft* (1781). Schleiermacher's brief reconstruction was as follows. "Knowing is a truth claim based on objective grounds. ... Belief [or faith] is a truth claim based on subjective grounds. ... There is a still higher truth claim based on subjective grounds, one that ... relates to the very subject making the truth claim. This is immediate self-consciousness. ... Finally, opinion can be either a subjective or an objective truth claim but is always accompanied by consciousness of the insufficiency of grounds." In his later thinking, faith of the kind presented in *Christian Faith* is identified with immediate self-consciousness.

the other side many an element bears the more complete form in itself. Also, since in time a coming to be out of nothing is inconceivable, there must indeed always already be something onto which the higher procedures of speculation can be tried, even if only a minimum. In no way, however, is the distinction such that one person is predestined to speculative knowing by virtue of one's nature, while another person is excluded from this. In everyone speculation exists as a power that can be raised to consciousness; it is one and the same stuff in everyone, both in what is crystallized in regularly shaped forms and in the raw crystal. Thus, everything that is some sort of knowing, even if only formally, rests on the absolute knowing now being sought and the principles of construction that it yields, and it is all brought forth by their power.

Lecture 6

We have to settle yet another difficulty. Someone could ask: How do we then intend to arrive at these supreme principles, since we surely cannot arrive at them otherwise than without them? Here everything that for the ancients constituted eristic[22] hinges on the fact that in order to come to know one must nonetheless have some prior knowing of that knowing. If one posits a specific differentiation between the principles of knowing and those of construction, it is difficult to get away from this quandary. One could perhaps avail oneself of a way out by exposing the nullity of one set of these principles, supposing that if this were false its contradiction would show up right soon, except that the construction of knowing is never completed and so as it is further executed this contradiction can become evident sooner or later.

If one takes what is transcendental and what is formal here to be one and the same, we answer that since the ground of original knowing and of every other knowing is the same, we cannot attribute to supreme knowing anything different than what the form of knowing is for any given knowing, also that we find in the latter the transcendentally and formally supreme knowing at the same time. Thus, our task is simply to analyze the idea of knowing overall. Now, one could perhaps say that without having supreme knowing we would indeed not know whether a particular is an example of knowing. Yet, for us all that appears simply as knowing is in that respect homogenous; to find what is absolute in particular cases of knowing we must indeed abstract directly from its content, so that what might possibly be in error does not enter into our investigation.

To be sure, the supposition that absolute knowing is contained in all particular cases of knowing does not possess the same dignity as the actual

---

22. Ed. note: As Arndt points out, Plato distinguished eristic, as the mode of persuasive argumentation used by the sophists, from dialectic.

knowing that is sought after, however necessary it may be to get a handhold on discovering this absolute. To this extent, we do see here the relative truth of the claim that belief stands above knowing; however, belief also rests on knowing insofar as knowing is an active ingredient in all our convictions.

As a force supreme knowing is the principle wherefrom every real knowing proceeds, however incomplete it may be; as something of which one is aware supreme knowing is the principle wherefrom science concerning what is real arises.

We then proceed from something recognized to be a knowing and in this knowing seek its principle. As was already said, we are going to look predominately at the formal aspect, yet without neglecting the transcendental aspect. Moreover, so as to fall into this latter danger as little as possible we will seek first to master the transcendental aspect and then seek at the same time to be aware that the transcendental aspect is coterminously the principle of the formal aspect and that what is absolute is coterminously the form of all knowing.

I. THE TRANSCENDENTAL PART

Knowing

Lecture 7

How is it that we recognize something to be an instance of real knowing?[23]
That is to say, there is much in us that is indeed analogous to knowing but is still

---

23. Ed. note: Here are Twesten's elaborations on this seventh lecture (Arndt, 89–90).

"How is it that something is recognized to be knowing?

"We place knowing as something particular under thinking as something general and thus inquire more definitely: How is it that an instance of thinking becomes one of knowing?

"As soon as we call an instance of thinking knowing, we assume a general validity of it for all thinkers. We do not recognize as an instance of knowing anything that fails to have this characteristic of general validity.

"For example, much can exist in us whereof we are convinced that we would never be able to think otherwise, as with maxims that constitute the expression of our individual existence; but we do not form the pretension that others are to think exactly in this way, and precisely on this account we do not call it knowing.

"If we communicate such an instance of knowing to someone else and are quite satisfied with our presentation, we intend and expect that this other person would form what is communicated into the person's own knowing. Now, we do indeed have this same aim also when we present an idea in a work of art, but in an entirely different way. The communication of our knowing is inclined toward the one to whom this is imparted producing the same knowing in the same way that we did. We make different claims on one who is observing a work of art, who must proceed in a way quite contrary to the way the artist proceeds, for in the artist a multiplicity of results has emerged from a simple point of departure whereas the observer must go back to what is simple from this multiplicity. We are convinced regarding our knowing that it is knowing even without our communication of it and would likely have arisen of itself in others purely by virtue of their reasoning nature. No one would believe this of a work of art. Knowing is generally valid even without communication, while in the case of art communication is necessary. The reason is this: Knowing is to arise not from the subjective, individual nature of any given person but is to arise from something general, human; in knowing we do indeed thus see something given in ourselves, but we are not then entrapped within the boundaries of personal existence but perceive within ourselves the knowing that is available to anyone.

"Here empirical skepticism confronts us with the following objection. To be sure, everyone has only one's own, and no one can know whether something in another is not viewed as knowing. Accordingly, we place knowing as something particular under thinking viewed in general terms. How is it that thinking becomes an instance of knowing? When a piece of thinking is posited as knowing we posit the general validity of this knowing for everything the action of which is comprised of that thinking. Whatever lacks this general validity we do not consider knowing. We have much within us regarding which we are conscious of never being able to think otherwise but without having the pretension that others too ought to think in this way. This kind of thing is not then knowing either—for example, maxims that apply to one's individual existence. When we communicate something to someone we would that the other might form as the other's own the same knowing that was previously in ourselves, supposing that we are satisfied with our communication. This is exactly how it is with art, but art is different from knowing. A communication of knowing has no other inclination than that the other persons shall produce that knowing in themselves. A work of art presumes otherwise: we do not intend that the onlooker do exactly the same as what we have done.[24] Thus, with respect to communication of knowing the conviction must not refer to the subjective nature of each person but must be based on what is purely human, and the communication has the goal of the other person's purely producing the same knowing. On this account, knowing has general validity even without its being communicated, while communication is necessary in art. Without this general validity there is no knowing. Thus, we are looking at something that exists in us, yet we are not restricted within the

---

analogous to what is present in oneself. Indeed, if one posits nothing held in common, for that person it is also the case that there is no knowing and the entire issue of what knowing would be is for that person vacuous. Yet, someone could say that at the same time every instance of real knowing still contains as well something mediated through our personal existence. We can grant that. It may be that in every instance of knowing that is present in any human consciousness there is alongside the generally valid element another element consisting of what is uncertain and individual. It may be that complete knowing is first attained only in the identity of the two and that precisely for the reason that what is sense-oriented is never purely absorbed into what is rational, complete knowing is eternally unachievable. In contrast, we abstract out a particular instance of knowing before all content, and there it must be permissible for us to undertake our investigation from the side of what is generally valid within it."

24. Ed. commentary: It may seem as though this statement is inconsistent with Schleiermacher's earlier identification of dialectic as a "work of art." It would indeed be so if he did not conceive dialectic as the supreme, all-encompassing art, one focused on shared knowing, versus that which is familiar to us within the aesthetic domain. Moreover, he regularly states of every domain that requires reflection that one must think matters out for oneself, but this view does not imply that everyone's expression or understanding possesses general validity, as is essential here and wherever dialectic applies. In the first hour of the 1814 lectures, he holds that every scientific person must do philosophy, if only to avoid entrapment in "traditional" positions, but that to philosophize without investigating matters scientifically will lead a person into "a dead, formalist scholasticism or into an immature, brooding mysticism."

boundaries of personal existence. In ourselves we see the knowing of some other person. Thus, it is spurious in this respect to take the inner phenomena of consciousness in such a way that they do not have general validity.

Empirical skepticism is directed against this view, objecting that each person has only what is one's own and that no one can know whether something analogous to it exists in another person. If someone does not posit anything held in common, that person also does not posit any knowing, and as a consequence the question does not arise for that person. — Yet, someone could say that every instance of real knowing nevertheless also contains, at the same time, something that is mediated through your own personal existence. However, our intention is to abstract something from the content of the knowing that is present; if the only thing that is present is something that has general validity, something that is unsettled or individual in nature may lie within our organs,[25] thus such material is knowing only through the other factor that we intend to search for. The identity of the two factors is what brings an instance of knowing to a complete status, yet on account of this it is also true that no finite knowing will reach that complete status. However, this does not keep us from being able to start our investigation based on the other aspect.

Lecture 8

Every bit of thinking, and thus knowing too, stands in relation both to the one who is thinking and to something that is thought of, to subject and object. What is thought of is something outside thinking but is given in the thinking. We have seen how the subject is posited in thinking insofar as it is a knowing. How is an instance of thinking, insofar as it is knowing, thought of in relation to its object?[26]

---

25. Ed. commentary: By "organs" Schleiermacher means whatever within the human body can be the locus of sense experience, not simply discrete organs such as the eyes or heart. In fact, in his psychology lectures and elsewhere he depicts the human "organism" as a more or less integrated body-mind, thus rejecting body/mind dualism. The "organic function" of which he will speak later in these lectures refers to this real experience of ourselves and the rest of nature through our organs, though not necessarily determined in full by sense-oriented experience. For example, philosophy is not so determined, nor are more advanced stages of religious consciousness.

26. Ed. note: From now on, grammatical features such as subject and object play a key role in Schleiermacher's presentation, for thinking that is knowing is ordinarily displayed, or is expressible, in sentences. Twesten's elaborations on the eighth lecture (Arndt, 90–92) are as follows.

"In every instance of thinking a relation to a subject is present. (We have seen, however, that if an instance of thinking is to be one of knowing, its subject would have to be not a particular *individuum*, not personal consciousness, but the totality of all personal existence, reason itself.) Likewise, in every instance of thinking there is a relation to an object,

What is the object that is posited outside thinking? When we think we are not only thinking but are thinking of something. What, then, is this something? Being. In every instance of thinking, what is thought is a knowing, what is known is a being. We cannot think except under the form of being, even if only

---

something thought of; and the question arises as to how an instance of thinking, insofar as it is to be one of knowing, is situated in relation to its object.

"In every instance of thinking, what is thought of is something outside the thinking yet given in thinking. In every instance of thinking or knowing, what is thought of or known is an instance of being. It is not possible to think of something otherwise than under the form of being, even if our thinking is an instance of sheer arbitrariness, of fantasizing or of error. The character of knowing consists in the congruence of thinking with being, with what is thought of.

"If we unite this feature with what was found earlier, that the subject of knowing is reason itself, knowing is thus the pure containment of reason in being. In that we place reason and being in relation to each other in this way, the congruence of the two seems to be necessary, for if one seeks to depart from the identity of the two, both the idea of being and that of reason disappear, and this is so, for there is a necessity in both that is expressed in the relation of the two to each other. Nothing can proceed from being that does not have its subjective grounding in reason as such. Error and arbitrariness cannot proceed from being. If it were conceivable that something would be different in reason than in being, both the idea of the necessity and orderliness of being and the reality of reason would disappear.

"Nevertheless, it does seem as if there are instances of knowing that do not refer to any object independent of knowing, namely:

"(1) In moral theory (*Sittenlehre*). On the one hand, we cannot deny the term "knowing" to the categorical imperative, for it is something valid in general. Yet, no being seems to correspond to it; rather, being seems first to be required by it. If no being actually corresponded to it, the categorical imperative would also be an empty fantasizing. However, insofar as a perception lies within it some being does correspond to it after all, namely that of reason. The categorical imperative expresses the formula for the action of reason, and only to this extent is it an instance of knowing. The exact same thing is the case here as with natural laws, which would also be precisely nothing but fantasy without the positing of nature.

"(2) In mathematics, the object of which seems to be produced only by thinking. The same thing holds here as well. If mathematics had no being as its object, it too would be empty fantasizing. However, mathematics receives its scientific character only through its relation to physics; what within it goes beyond being is a sheer point of transition, for the sake of returning to being.

"This objection has had to do merely with the formal aspect of our understanding. What follows seizes upon what is material as well.

"As it seems, in that we posit a being that is independent of knowing, we remove in advance that which should be the result of our investigation into whether things then exist and what they are. This objection is merely a seeming one. When one asks whether things then exist, one can mean two things thereby. (a) Simply whether there is then an instance of knowing. Already from this question one sees that one cannot get away from having the concept of being, pretend though one will. (b) Whether knowing is congruent with the thing. In the first place, this need not yet trouble us at all. If things are different from what we think they are, no instance of knowing is even present; however, knowing is and remains the pure congruence of the two. What is subjective has its necessary correlative in what is objective. However, how we might be able to discover whether a congruence between the two exists in a given instance of knowing does not yet trouble us; rather, this can happen only at the end of our investigation."

in and for ourselves. Even in arbitrary thinking, in fantasizing, what is thought takes on the form of being, and it is not otherwise in the case of error, for we implicate error too with the being of what is thought to the degree that it is a true thought.

Through what relation to being does an instance of thinking become one of knowing? In not knowing, being is a mere form of our thinking; in error too we refer thinking to some being independent of it, but there thinking does not relate to its being as thinking is supposed to relate to being. For example, if in thinking a false predicate is attributed to being, it is not such in being. Knowing is the congruence of thinking with being as what is thought.

Now, in addition: Knowing is never simply a personal consciousness but is the totality of all personal existence and is therewith reason itself. Thus, knowing is the pure coinciding of reason with being. In that we place reason and being over against each other, the congruence of the two seems necessary. Nothing can proceed from being as such than what also has its subjective grounding in reason as such. Error and arbitrariness have never proceeded from being. If one tries to diverge from this identity between the two, the ideas of being and reason will be lost to us, for in each of them there is a necessity that is expressed in the relation of each to the other. If it were conceivable that there is something different in reason than in being, the idea of the necessity of being would be lost and its lawlike character. Even the reality belonging to reason would be lost in this case. What we find instead is a reciprocal action in which both endure.[27]

---

27. Ed. commentary: This is a critically important passage. Pervading it is a deep trust in the ideal correspondence between being and thinking, in the worthwhileness of thinkers' stretching out toward being and in their ultimate success. This trust becomes an underlying commitment, aware of difficulties, some of which Schleiermacher is already beginning to mention here, but unshakable. Some have argued that to hold to this commitment in the face of all the multiplicity, fragmentariness, unpredictable change and uncertainty in the world is to persist in a conservative fantasy. To be radically, sensibly "postmodern," for example, would mean to repudiate this faulty "modern" assumption.

An argument intended to support such a claim would be that social and political institutions have used this assumption to imagine that reality is contained in neat little boxes and to keep people's lives captive there. Counter to this argument is the steady example of Schleiermacher himself, whose ways of meeting and affirming all the characteristics of the world just mentioned, as of our equally extensive human inadequacies, lead to an extraordinarily progressive latitude and flexibility with respect to both methods and institutions. It is precisely this drive to attain overall, interconnected meaning, while honoring the singularity and distinctiveness of individual cases, that enables him to entertain so many new possibilities in every domain.

Since its beginnings, the modern age has seen the heightening of ancient controversies over whether "being" can truly be known, because it is accessible to human minds and displays an orderliness in its processes, or whether human limitations are too great and "being" too unstable and disparate for it to be fathomable, or whether "being" gives itself to be known at all. Along a wide spectrum of views, Schleiermacher's position resides in the first direction.

Yet, in the ethical and in the mathematical domains it seems that much appears as knowing wherein nothing that is thought is present as referring to something independent of knowing. For example, the categorical imperative, the moral law, is indeed an instance of knowing, for it is something general and is combined with conviction, but no being independent of it seems to correspond to it but only one that is first to arise with it. If it should be the case that no being corresponds to this thinking, it would be fantasy; but insofar as some perception[28] is lodged within it, a true being does correspond to the perception. If that being is something real, it must be something. We posit reason as a kind of being, and the categorical imperative expresses the formula as to how reason operates, and only to that extent is it an instance of knowing. The same is true of natural laws: if nature is not posited there, these laws are likewise nothing but fantasy.

No being seems to correspond to what is thought in mathematical knowing either; rather, being is first produced through the thinking. Arithmetic and geometry are also not as yet true knowing at all. Geometry contains curves and matters of degree in its various possible syntheses. How do we arrive at such constructions? It is the movement involved that does it. Mathematics has its scientific character simply through its reference to mathematics. What proceeds beyond being there is at a sheer point of transition, only to return to being. In the actual domain where it is used some being does of course belong to it.

Still, in that we posit involvement with things, it appears as if we are removing the result of our investigation in advance. This objection is merely a seeming one. When one asks whether given things exist one can only mean to ask whether those things and knowing are congruent[29] with each other or whether what we have is simply knowing. Here one does not get away from being, and if things are also of a different nature from what we think they are, no knowing is

---

In no small part, however, the genius of his dialectic lies in its readiness to deal honestly with limitations that become so markedly noticeable as one moves in the second direction. This will, I think, become apparent as he proceeds here. The same spirit suffuses his complementary work on hermeneutics and criticism.

28. *Anschauung.* Ed note: This term has several levels of usage in Schleiermacher's thinking, from equivalence to *Wahrnehmung* (sense perception) to an outward tending perspective paired with the inward oriented *Gefühl* (feeling), to an overall grasp of our perspective on the universe. Here the level is indeterminate. *Anschauung* is an activity of *Gemüth* (mind and heart) that literally "looks upon" something out there, as it were. That something is "posited" (*gesetzt*) as existing, on the basis of evidence. Thus, the word "intuition," often used for *Anschauung,* is avoided here, because of the distracting connotation of a special capacity that is either wholly separable from ordinary sense perception (*Wahrnehmung*) or merely subjective or purely anticipatory and prophetic or some mixture among the three.

29. *Kongruieren.* Ed. note: See also just below: *Kongruenz.* Here the thought is of something like mere, superimposed coincidence in mathematics; no natural or necessary connection is as yet present.

present and for this reason knowing indeed remains a matter of pure congruence. A subject necessarily has a correlate in its object. We still do not know how we can find out whether congruence is present in a given instance of knowing. When knowing comes to nothing being does too.

Thinking

Lecture 9

Knowing is a thinking that is posited with its general validity. What is thinking?[30] Every instance of thinking arises from two elements, a formal element and a material element. As to the latter: every instance of thinking rests on an organic function. As to the first: this organic function is assumed in a form such that through it an instance of knowing emerges or the opposite of such an

---

30. Ed. note: See Jonas's summary on thinking from a student transcript in SW III.4:2 (1839), 56f and 315f. Here is Twesten's elaboration on this ninth lecture (Arndt, 92–93).

"Knowing is thinking posited with general validity. Every instance of thinking, however, consists of two elements, a material element and a formal one. The material element of an instance of thinking is comprised of a certain organic function. The formal element is the reception of the material element in a form such that through it an instance of knowing arises or the opposite of knowing.

"A purely formal instance of thinking, one lacking in organic function, cannot occur at all. What may seem to be such is, in part, simply something that refers to something that preceded it, in that, for example, it combines several acts of thought, which have themselves contained an organic function, into one act of thought; in part, it is simply an apparatus preliminary to becoming an instance of knowing and will only become such an instance once I will have filled the empty form with something organic. If, for example, I say "a = a" ("a" considered to be a sign of something observed), this expression is of course entirely formal, but it will also become a vital instance of knowing only when I insert into the "a" something that has arisen from an organic function. Moreover, this purely formal thinking has also arisen only from acts of thought that contain an organic function, and has perhaps not preceded them in one's consciousness. The acts of thought wherein alone an instance of knowing can exist in this vital way is called 'perception', in contrast to sheer formal thinking.

"In view of the relationship between the formal and material elements, two cases are then possible. Either every organic operation accompanies a particular formal element, one that is appropriate only to it, and every formal combination has its particular organic function, or every formal element is able to encompass and permeate the entire material domain, and every material element is permeated by every formal element. Patently, the latter is the case, for otherwise we would not even have been able to make this distinction. Now, if an instance of thinking is to be one that has general validity, as knowing is to be, then not only must the identity of the formal element, the unity of reason, be posited in all thinkers but that which is the work of the organic function in that same instance of thinking must also be able to persist with the knowing of every other thinker, must be able to be an extension of that thinking. To that extent, every thinker is considered to be a member in the system of organic functions, just as reason can be a subject of knowing only in its respective identity in all."

instance. Through the first element knowing becomes something singular, a distinct knowing.

One could object that there is such a thing as a purely formal thinking without any organic function; that would be an instance of thinking about nothing, and such cannot at all be present as referring to something that precedes it. For example, in "a = a" no organic function is in evidence, except insofar as this is nothing but a combining of several thoughts that have an organic function into one single function, and this would then be the formal element common to several acts of real thought. In itself, such thinking is also vacuous and signifies something only to the extent that one is thinking of something different that is posited therein. Every sentence of this sort presupposes prior acts of thought. However, not all sentences by which something is asserted and in which the physical presence of things is lacking are such that organic functions are missing in them.

Now, in contrast, there are also things that are so-called matters of understanding. General concepts, for example that of "oven," are already of this kind. Here it may seem as though it is the same as when the organic function is lacking; but this is mere semblance, for this is something that is brought forth from a thing into the senses and is in no way something that does not belong to the nature of the thing (indeed, an oven should produce a rise in temperature). And so it is overall. If a sentence is not vacuous, we posit organic function with it. For example, this is the case when one asserts something of an animal, for "animal" is either a purely vacuous expression, a sign like the letter "a," or one posits therewith all possible forms in which the nature of animals is revealed to our senses, and only in this way does the word have any life to it.

An instance of thinking that is formal can never be one of knowing but is only a preliminary apparatus for becoming an instance of knowing. It can become an instance of knowing only in that what is vacuous is (1) filled in and (2) organic function is also constantly present within it, even if in a minimal way. These acts in which it is possible for an instance of knowing to exist are called "perception," in contrast to thinking, which, however, simply rests on perception as if thinking subsisted precisely in the opposite.

In our concept of knowing lies the presupposition that reason, the highest potency of consciousness, is the same in everyone. Now, if one instead posits formal and organic operation as different from each other, one can say that there exists a manifoldness of combinations and one of organic functions. In that case, either a particular combination is peculiar to each organic function or it is possible for several thoughts to issue from each one; further, either each combination has its particular organic function or no formal element has its particular material element. In contrast, it is rather the case that every formal element can embrace the entire realm of organic functions, and vice versa. Otherwise it would not even be possible to make such a distinction. In every instance of thinking its form is the principle of unity, its sensory component is the principle of manifoldness. Thus, any material element you like can become a member of some different combination, and every formal element can encompass many organic functions. For example, the sense perception of most colors or the organic element in the sentence "the oven is hot" could have occasioned various instances of knowing; further, the fixing of a certain sense perception upon an object can repeatedly recur in relation to a great many varied elements of material thinking. Thus, any one of these can exist in combination with a multiplicity of others. So, in every instance of knowing it is not merely a matter of the formal element's being in accord with the organic element; viewed from the side of the organic element as well, the one must be in accord with the other and engender it. Without this the reception of a piece of knowing is null and void. The knowing of each person must be able to cohere with the knowing of every other person, and what is on the one hand the unity of reason is on the other hand the sum total of all organic functions. Absolute knowing can become real only in its uniting with the organic element, and just as reason can be a subject of knowing only in its identity in all subjects, from the side of the organic element knowing can then be an instance of knowing only insofar as each instance belongs to the system of organic function, is a member of that system. The identity of all possible perception becomes exhaustive only in knowing.

Lecture 10

The entire domain of the organic elements of knowing must form a unity, whereof a certain formal element is its center and the organic elements are the periphery, and vice versa. Thus, only a piece of knowing is to be found in each real instance of knowing, and the entirety of knowing exists only in its wholeness.[31]

---

31. Ed. note: See Jonas's summary from a student transcript, in SW III.4:2 (1839), p. 316. Here is Twesten's elaboration from his own notes (Arndt, 94).

"The entirety of knowing consists in the uniting of the entire domain of organic elements around each formal element conceived as the periphery around their centrum, also in the permeating of the entire domain of formal elements by every material element. Every instance of real knowing, however, is simply a piece of this whole, a whole that through the identity of the formal and material domains must be able to persist with and alongside every other instance and be able to complete it.

"The second characteristic of knowing mentioned was the correspondence of thinking with some being. Now, all thinking is either concept or judgment (for the conclusion is not a primary form but is only a combination of the two). Yet, both forms mutually presuppose each other. Thus, what we seem to have here is a knowing that consists in two mutually

An organic element is present even in ethical concepts such as "justice," for such a concept proceeds from perceptions of inner sensibility, from perceptions of pleasure and the lack of pleasure, and of action that attaches itself to them.

The second characteristic of knowing was thinking's corresponding with some being. Now, all thinking is comprised of either concept or judgment. A conclusion is but a combination of these other two features and does not constitute a primary form. The forming of a concept is an act of thinking all its own; through that act some being, some unity of being, is established, and this is in and of itself an act of thinking. In contrast, judgment is a combination, in that something is asserted by a subject. The two forms mutually presuppose each other, however. The reason is that a concept contains several judgments, into which the concept is also broken down, for example in the interest of trying to make a concept clear to someone else. If we should lay out a history of a given concept, we would be able to show how it arose in various stages and how it did so based on which particular judgments. Yet, we may ask: How can an instance of knowing arise if concepts and judgments presuppose each other? If all knowing appears as mutually implicated, where is the initial point of departure? There must be an identity of the two that itself must be the source of all real knowing, thus its absolute, and this source cannot be either concept or judgment but must be the pure identity of the two.[32]

---

implicated features, where one can rightly inquire as to its primitive point of departure. This primitive point of departure can be neither concept nor judgment but must be the identity of the two and thus belong to what is absolute, the source of all real knowing. We search for this point of departure by proceeding first from concept and then from judgment."

32. Ed. commentary: Here, as throughout most of these lectures, the presentation must be followed very closely and each part held almost visually in mind to be understood. Here Schleiermacher is claiming a holistic perspective. In doing so, he is presupposing that the whole of nature, in fact of all possible being, is interconnected. This whole, however, cannot be accessed from any one point by thinking, which cannot itself ever be complete, cannot reach its end, until it has grasped that whole. Thus, the whole of reality cannot be mirrored from one place, by a single observer. Along the way to complete, fully integrated knowing, concepts are formed, and these provisionally capture some part of the whole and of relationships among entities and events within it. Integral to the forming of concepts, also to their use for description or explanation, is the entry of judgments. Once judgments are in the picture, they are interdependent with concepts.

Judgments are comprised of people's discriminations (it would seem either as to what is the case or as to what is important—facts and values, and always inextricably interdependent) in comparison with contrasting qualities, things, categories, and more. Judgments serve, in this way, to combine various aspects of our experience with each other, such as observations. Schleiermacher seems to be imagining all this activity's eventually entering into sentences, or at least incomplete components of sentences. Conclusions to an argument do not make up a third category of thinking, he holds, because they do not add anything substantive that is not already present in the sentences used as premises, namely concepts and judgments placed in that form. Later on here, Schleiermacher will discuss other elements of sentences that enable them to say something, particularly those elements that represent action.

A concept is a hovering between what is general and what is particular, for in part it comprehends a particular that is manifold, and what is empirical and individual is subsumed under it as a unity. On the other hand, it is itself subsumable under something higher. For example, the lower concept "sweet" can be subsumed under higher concepts referring to the activity of the organ involved. For every concept there are lower ones that are to be subsumed under it and higher ones under which it is to be subsumed. Where does this come to an end? Reaching a lowest level of a concept never happens. For example, what is subordinated under the concept "sweet" permits of being set forth as a concept over and over again if we are but acquainted with what is internal to the operation that belongs to a concept. Hence, we attach to the end of every concept the possibility of a plurality of judgments that would define it still further.

The highest concept is that of that thing, of being in general, in which nothing more is then distinguished that would make a subsumption under something higher possible. Yet, actually this is then no longer a concept, because of the two relations that make up every concept only one is left. Nevertheless, in the highest concept we still have a contrast between concept and object. We no more think of the concept without this contrast than it is the case that the contrast is to be regarded as an instance of knowing. The contrast is, however, the form that belongs to a judgment. Thus, at the very apex of the forming of concepts stands a judgment, but even this judgment, in turn, presupposes a concept. Thus, what is supreme is the identity of being and thinking, of the concept and the thing, since I dissolve that judgment therein; yet, no contrast between thinking and what is thought exists here any longer, only the identity of the two. On the other hand, this is the supreme transcendent knowing, for it stands above both the ethical and the physical domains, and it is the supremely formal feature of knowing, since it is concept and judgment at the same time. This knowing, in turn, determines all individual knowing, which without this identity is incomplete.

It is also useful to recall at this point that all the presentations Schleiermacher makes in his account of dialectic are intended to serve the "conducting of conversation" (*Gesprächs-führung*), hence the heavy emphasis on features of grammar and syntax. His moves are always closely in touch with that sphere, and he wishes to show as much the continuity between ordinary and scholarly language as their various discontinuities, though he typically does not stop here to reveal any preliminary analyses of language that he would have performed. Likewise, he does not drift far from his aim to account for the organization of science as a whole, though he does not typically stop here to reveal difference among its branches that he would have reflected about. He does share something of these respective analyses and reflections in other, more particular contexts, however, and speaks of how they have been and are situated historically.

Lecture 11

We have seen that every concept is a synthesis of something higher and something lower, a hovering between the two.[33] The first must be a unity, while the second must be an absolute manifoldness,[34] because the process of

---

33. Ed. note: See Jonas's summary from a student transcript in SW III.4:2 (1839), p. 316. Twesten's elaboration on his own notes here is as follows (Arndt, 95–96).

"A concept is something that hovers between something general and something particular. This is so in that for every concept there is something lower that is subordinate to it and something higher under which it is subsumable. If one searches out the two respective ends, one finds that one cannot arrive at a lowest level of a concept, for at that lowest point we still attach the possibility of infinitely numerous judgments that could define it still more fully, thus we could still see the possibility of many lower concepts. The supreme concept, however, is that of the thing, of being, because herein there does not appear to be any further manifold that would make a subsumption under something higher possible. Yet, even here there is still a contrast between the concept of the thing and the object of the concept; thus, still here, at the apex of the formation of concepts, there is a judgment that presses us to go higher. Accordingly, the highest we can go is the identity of being and thinking, of concept and thing, an identity in which the contrast between thinking and what is thought disappears. This highest point, as positioned above the ethical and the physical domains, is the supreme, transcendent knowing; as positioned above concept and judgment, it is the supreme formal knowing; and it is determinative of all individual instances of knowing.

"Judgment is the synthesis of some being and some nonbeing or a hovering between the two. This is so, for every judgment is the combination of a subject and a predicate, but to the extent that these require combination they are set over against judgment, are different. Thus, to the extent that a subject is present in a judgment, the subject is posited as not being that which is attributed to it but at the same time is posited as being (for otherwise nothing could be predicated of it), so judgment consists in the identity of being and nonbeing.

"The subject is posited as something that exists in and of itself. However, what can be predicated of it is not the subject. The measure of the subject is thus the minimum of that which can be predicated of it. Accordingly, the supreme subject is that of which nothing can be predicated, thus being, for of this subject one can indicate only that it exists; that, however, is a judgment of identity, one that expresses nothing real unless that be precisely that here all predicating comes to a halt.

"In contrast, in itself the predicate has no being at all, it has this only in something else. Thus, it has the more being the more subjects to which it can be predicated and supreme being if it can be predicated of everything. To the sphere of these predicates corresponds the sphere of the most minimal subjects, or the domain of absolute becoming in contrast to that of absolute being."

34. *Eine absolute Mannigfaltigkeit.* Ed. commentary: The word "absolute" in this singular phrase means total, unexcepted chaos, not ordered (that is, no "comprehending," or fastening together or comprehension of things—on "chaos" see the 25th, 43d and 46th lectures). This usage serves to remind us that Schleiermacher, unlike Schelling and some other of his contemporaries, never hypostatizes *das absolute* or *das Absolute* (translated both "what is absolute" and "the absolute," depending on the context). The term does not refer to a single being, though he does identify the concept "absolute" with the concept "God" or "deity" as supreme being (*das Höchste*, in the Bible "the Highest," or *das höchste Sein*), the fundament of all thinking, and "as transcendent being, the principle of all being and as transcendent idea the formal principle of all knowing," but, as he says, nothing more is to be said of it in dialectic

comprehending begins with it. The supreme subsumption could not be comprised by the concept of a concept, because what is supreme must not be able to be viewed as a result of judgment, and this is so because then a manifold would be present within it. The end that the concept achieves from below could not be exhausted by a quantity of judgments. What is supreme, on account of its being a unity, could not be comprised under the form of a concept insofar as it is the product of a judgment. Here we view it only from the formal side and thus not completely; we must also observe it from another side. In every instance of knowing, however, what is supreme is what makes it into such an instance. What is supreme is the identity of concept and judgment. In and of itself, every concept appears as something arbitrary; one cannot, however, rest with a judgment; the identity of the two, of which one becomes conscious at the level of what is supreme, makes it into an instance of knowing.

Judgment is a synthesis of being and nonbeing, or a hovering between the two that is defined by the fact that each is something determinate. Judgment consists of subject and predicate. Both are concepts, for insofar as I make some individual into a subject this is no judgment, for at that point one is not sure whether another person likewise construes the individual as something infinite so that the subject remains purely one. Judgment is the combination of the two. Insofar as the two are combined in a judgment, prior to the judgment they are different, contrasted to each other; the subject is continually posited as something that exists, if one would predicate something of it, and the predicate is similarly posited. Judgment then rests on the fact that in and of itself the subject is not what is attributed to it as a predicate; thus, the subject is not all that can be predicated of it. Further, then, every judgment is an identity of being and nonbeing, for being is the subject and nonbeing the predicate. Every determinate judgment thus rests on two extreme points. The subject is posited as something existent in and of itself but also as not being (insofar as this is posited in judgment) what can be attributed to it. Thus, as minimum point of predicating, the subject has no measure. The supreme entity is, accordingly, that of which, if a subject is posited, nothing can be predicated; this, however, is the point at which judgment turns into concept. A supreme entity of which nothing but its being can be predicated is thus one judged to be identical. Such a judgment of identity, however, is also nothing real, contrary to what "supreme subject" would express, for of this supreme entity nothing but its being can be predicated. A predicate is posited as something that exists in something else. Thus, it has only

---

(23d lecture). Rather, the term functions similarly to the way the ultimate "being of all that is" and "the good" do in Plato's thought or, to a lesser extent, to the way *telos* does in Aristotle's metaphysics. Note the contrast of "absolute unity" and "absolute manifoldness" at the close of this lecture.

so much existence as it is applied to something else that exists, the moreso the more there are of these. It would have supreme existence if it could be predicated of all subjects. If a predicate can be predicated of all subjects, one also posits only subjects that are in turn themselves predicates, which can in turn be applied to all subjects. These are the two terminus points of judgment, and it is something determinate insofar as it can be contained between them. Thus, the two terminus points are these: (1) absolute being, of which nothing can be predicated except its being; (2) absolute predication, according to which every subject is only relatively a subject and can also be a predicate.

On the one hand, a concept may apply to a supreme entity, in which the contrast between the being and the thinking of one who exists is resolved; nothing else can also be the supreme subject. The formation of concepts has had its terminus in something indeterminate, because at this point a concept is possible only through an infinite set of judgments. The identical terminus of judgments lies at the point where everything is equally subject and predicate, thus has no being of itself, where there is an identity of being and nonbeing, so that no subject can be established as something continuous (what, in contrast to being, is designated by the term "becoming").

Until this juncture, we have considered thinking only as thinking viewed purely apart from knowing. All that has been said goes only to the form of concept and that of judgment. Thus, what we have now found is the principle of thinking in general terms. Every formation of a concept proceeds from absolute unity and absolute manifoldness. Even if unconsciously, this is the guiding principle in every operation of thinking. If we consider thinking under the form of knowing, this must happen in an even more definite way.

Identity of Knowing and Being under the Aspect
of the Formation of Concepts

Lecture 12

The supreme being of subject and predicate that was finally lit upon was found by thinking and is thus also a general form of thinking as such.[35]

In that we are to apply what was found by thinking to the second characteristic of knowing, thus also to the domain of judgment, we seem to be justifying the positing of an individual thing as such.

Two objections may be lodged against this conclusion.

---

35. Ed. note: From here to the end of these 1811 lectures, the main text consists only of Schleiermacher's own preliminary notes.

The first objection is offered under the common form of skepticism. That is to say: One could not predicate anything in particular except organic function and would indeed not know what lies at the basis of this organic function in things. One could not posit knowing and being as comparable, because they are separated precisely in the domain of the real.

The first answer is as follows. The identity of being and knowing would be posited in the absolute. This answer, however, presupposes that the construction of science has reached completion and that in their derivation from the absolute, knowing and being have always remained parallel.

The second answer is this. The identity of concept and object would also be a presentation that proceeds from a concept. This presentation provides warranty for that notion. The skeptic who would give up knowing but would preserve thinking wants to preserve the traffic with things that falls entirely within this presentation. Thus, the skeptic must grant the identity of concept and object.

Lecture 13

The second objection arises from the combining of two contrasting outlooks.

The first outlook is the idealistic one. There all thinking would be based on the identity of concept and object. The first form of thinking would be the concept, but the individual thing would not be wholly contained in the concept, so that this same thing could be a nonbeing and an identity of thinking and what is thought. In this relation there could be no character of knowing; rather, there would be no knowing concerning this identity but instead knowing would simply be the absolute and whatever derivation is made therefrom.

The second outlook is the empirical one. There the individual thing, viewed as direct being, would not be wholly contained in the concept, so that this concept too would not have the form of knowing. Empirical knowing would consist of judgments concerning individual things.

Now, since the first outlook annuls the empirical outlook and the second outlook annuls the idealistic outlook, if the two are combined all knowing comes to be annulled.

The answer is that, first, one can also say that the empirical outlook is posited by the idealistic outlook and the formal outlook is posited by the empirical outlook, so that if the two are combined everything is posited. Second, one would then have to say that each of these two outlooks is simply onesided. (1) In its thesis, the empirical outlook denies the concept, but in practice it assumes the concept, for the combination without which it does not effectuate any judgment is given to it as a concept. (2) In its thesis, the idealistic outlook denies the organic function, but in practice it assumes the organic function; this is so, for it cannot construe the manifold belonging to a subordinate concept as a concept, rather it must thus come forth as something individual by means of the organic function.

So, the objection is only a support for the identity between the unity of what is absolute, on the one hand, and the totality of all particulars, on the other, that we have laid down as our basis here.

Lecture 14

Each of the two outlooks is of itself incomplete and produces no instance of knowing.

The idealistic outlook ever hovers between cognition and invention.

At the lower end of cognition, the empirical outlook satisfies itself with memoranda for use in the traffic with things.

Thus, it necessarily follows that being that is not wholly contained in concept, the being of individual things, is not the whole of being.

It also necessarily follows that construction based on the supreme concept purely by means of derivation is not the only knowing.

Sense perception and construction posited as identical yields a higher perception, for which precisely this is the formula: that thinking corresponds to being.

Accordingly, the contrast between higher and lower must also be found in being as in the concept.

To the higher concepts corresponds a higher being and a truer being, because less nonbeing is posited in it.

The supreme being is that which is at the same time its concept, that under which all else is subsumed, just as lower concepts are subsumed under higher concepts.

Lecture 15

Addenda to the Last Hour:

1. It has been said that the statement that some being would correspond to general concepts insofar as they are instances of knowing comprises the theory of ideas. One could conclude from this that concept and idea are to be distinguished.

In Plato, *eidos*, *idea* and *genos* are synonymous. The first two refer to form, the third to kind.[36] Thus, the first two refer to the common element in the individual, the third to the unity of productive power, and all three are posited alike in their synonymous usage.[37] — "Concept" designates the subjective mode of originating, higher being viewed as given with sense perception of lower being, the act of comprehending. Within such a concept there still remains the possibility of something false being present. In contrast, as an instance of knowing "concept" is equivalent to "idea."

2. "God" is no postulate that would have to be given so as actually to effectuate real knowing. One could have no real knowing at all, or no means whatsoever to distinguish knowing from not knowing in individual cases, and certitude as to God would be unaltered because this certitude lies in the very idea of knowing.[38]

3. The "presentation" referred to here is no demonstration. Demonstration presupposes acknowledgment of something else, but cognition of God is the original cognition that underlies all other cognition.

Lecture 16
(Monday, June 10)

The being of types[39] does not exist outside the being of kinds and of individual things; rather it exists in and with them, and they exist through it.

---

36. *Geschlecht.*

37. Ed. note: On these comparisons, see Schleiermacher's 1812 history of philosophy lectures, SW III.4:1 (1839), p. 103f: "Now, as dialectic leads to physics throughout, so in order to understand physics correctly one must also begin with dialectic and indeed with the theory of ideas, that is to say the theory that the unity of the concept is at the same time the true, real being in relation to the plurality of things, what is original (*urbildlich*) in relation to what is modeled after it (*abbildlich*). In the first relation the same thing has more the name *eidos*, in the latter relation more the name *idea*; then, precisely in these two relations the productive power of nature as such, the *paradeigma* for the forming (*Bildung*) of phenomena in their becoming, and physically it is termed the true *on* [being]."

38. Ed. note: On the idea of "God," see the 1812 history of philosophy lectures, SW III.4:1 (1839), p. 103: In regard to dialectic, the way Socrates and Plato "arrived at the idea of deity certainly shows that every Hellenic philosophy has to be theistic, since theism already emerged through its sheer polemic against skeptical antiphilosophical thinking. Moreover, this is just as certainly the triumph of philosophy, for to have to call upon the deity as something alien for assistance in explaining nature or forming moral laws is always short of the mark and degrading of science." As Arndt indicates, these remarks support the opposition (stated in the main text) to using "God" as a postulate in an account either of pure or of practical reason, as Kant did.

39. *Gattungen.*

Thus, thinking about types and kinds is an instance of knowing only to the extent that at the same time the productivity of what is particular within it is also posited along with what is general within it.

In being at the lowest level this occurs as an indeterminate repeatability of uniform production, in being at the higher levels as a cycling of a determinate manifoldness of modifications in production.

The being of kinds and types exists only through that of the higher levels.

Thus, thinking about them is also an instance of knowing only to the extent that what is particular in their being is posited as a more precise determination of what is higher (and, in whatever circumstances, posited as with its coordinates).

The being of individual things exists only through that of kinds, and only in that way is each of them some one thing.

Thus, even in notions regarding these entities, if they are to be instances of knowing the concept of kind must be co-posited, and only in this way does the notion of an individual participate in the form of a concept.

Hence, we must have concepts before we have notions of individual things as such. This is an indirect presentation of the theory of innate concepts.[40]

Lecture 17

Addenda:

(1) What has been said applies equally well to the ethical as to the physical domain. In the ethical domain too, knowing under the form of concept can be only such a living perception.[41]

(2) Thus, the scaffolding of all ethical and physical knowing is erected through what has been set forth, for all existing forms must be contained in this system of concept formation. Moreover, an implication of this point is that none of these forms is to be fully understood independent of the entire system to which it belongs. Indeed, not even the concept of physical knowing can be fully understood without that of ethical knowing, and vice versa.

---

40. Ed. note: The presentation is indeed "indirect," for Schleiermacher gives no evidence of subscribing to a full-flung theory of innate ideas (read: *angebornen* for *angebohrnen*), as was advanced in Plato's theory of knowing as recollection or in later rationalist views. In the 1814 lectures on dialectic (#176.4) he states: "This timeless precedence of all concepts in reason is what is true in the theory of innate concepts, insofar as this theory opposes that which views all concepts simply as secondary products based on organic affection." What is true in a theory, of course, does not constitute the theory in its entirety, nor is a theory identifiable simply in terms of that.

41. Ed. note: See the third lecture, above. Through the great humanistic thinker and Schleiermacher interpreter, Wilhelm Dilthey (1833–1911), the ethical domain came to be called *Geisteswissenschaften* (today: "the human sciences").

(3) If the individual thing at the lowest level of concept is also to be understood only under the form of indeterminate plurality, the productive power of any kind is, as a quantum, to be removed from terms of a more or less, and this too contributes toward the completeness of knowledge.

(4) What has been set forth is knowing in its completion, except that it is present only as something that is becoming. The concept of a type is prior to an insight as to how it is created through kinds. Thus, up to that point kinds are represented only as individual things and observation is counterposed to construction, though so that neither kinds nor observations ever form an instance of knowing of themselves but do this only in concert. In pure knowing, however, each exists in the other, and, based on varied points of view, the knowing is either philosophical or historical.[42]

What is absolute is not to be thought of as a singular thing that is exhausted only in an infinity of judgments; nor is it to be thought of as a concept caught in the identity between a lower and a higher concept. Its concept also cannot exist outside what is absolute itself. We can have what is absolute only granted the inadequacy of any image of deity we have in the identity of our being and our concept. There is no such thing as an isolated perception of deity. Rather, we perceive the deity only in and with the collective system of perception. The deity is just as surely incomprehensible as the knowledge of it is the basis of all knowledge. Exactly the same is true also on the side of feeling.[43]

*Identity of Knowing and Being under the Aspect
of the Formation of Judgments*

Lecture 18

Our knowing concerning God is thus completed only with our perspective on the world.[44] As soon as a trace of the latter exists, the basic features of the former make their appearance as well. To the degree that a perspective on the

---

42. *Historisches.*

43. Ed. note: Here and in the eighteenth lecture Schleiermacher refers directly to his identical analysis in *On Religion* (1799, revised edition in 1806). Formally, this analysis, which in sum is consistent with that in the lectures on dialectic, had a great impact on his presentation of doctrine in *Christian Faith* one and two decades later, for there God is not taken to be directly knowable (thus, not in God's own being or internal relations, if there be any), or even directly perceived or felt, but is so only through the interconnected system of nature, in both its physical and its ethical aspects.

44. *Weltanschauung.*

world is defective the idea of deity remains mythical. Alternatively, if it is nonetheless separated from having a perspective on the world and is at the same time to be brought under the strict form of thinking, it is untenable. (True atheism exists only in union with positive skepticism. Every other form of atheism is simply directed against what is untenable and mythical.)

For now, this is as far as we go regarding concept formation. Now we go on to discuss judgment: that is to say, how being is posited in judgment and thus how it has to be so posited if a judgment is to be an instance of knowing.

The form of judgment has reality only where subject and predicate considered in themselves as concepts are in no way identical. Thus, it is not possible for judgments to show how being is posited in them where the subject itself is in turn posited as predicate or where the predicate is the next higher concept for the subject or is an indicator of this next higher concept.

Subject and predicate are presupposed to be different, but in judgment they are bound in one inseparable unity. This is done, however, in such a way that this unity is divided in that a number of judgments is possible for one subject and is subordinate to the unity and the being-of-itself of the subject. The being posited in a judgment is thus a lower one as compared to that in the concept of the subject involved, relating to it as what is changing to what is constant, as what is arbitrary to what is essential. Thus, the being posited in a judgment is not peculiar to the given subject but is rather a being common to it and another subject. The original expression for the predicate is the verb, thus the condition of action or passivity, the possibility for which is indeed posited in the concept of the subject but its actuality rests on its being-in-common with others.

In actual concepts (general things) nothing is arbitrary and changing; rather, only what is essential and remains self-identical[45] is posited. Thus, they are not actually the subjects of judgment.

The actual domain of judgments is comprised of individual, particular things, and all else takes part in that domain only to the extent that it is represented under this form.

Transitive and intransitive judgments express different degrees of commonality.[46]

---

45. *Sich selbst gleich bleibende.*

46. Ed. note: See note 57 below. In an earlier paragraph just above, "being-in-common" translates *Zusammensein* (which could also mean co-existence or commonality); here, as there, "commonality" translates *Gemeinschaft*. — In grammar "transitive" refers to "passing over" to an object or expressing an action as not restricted to the subject involved but still directed to

Lecture 19
(Monday, June 17)

So, judgment may appear to be the form of empirical knowing, and general things may appear to belong under judgment only to the extent that they are still apprehended empirically because they fall short of completed construction. Thus, judgment may appear to be merely a supplement to concept that should gradually disappear.

However, being is present within organic function always and only in activity; and if even after the contrast between a priori and a posteriori is lifted, the twofold form of cognition, the philosophical and the historical,[47] remains, the first form being represented through concepts and the latter through judgments.

Thus, judgment has a validity all its own and only in it and concept together does completed knowing take place.

Accordingly, even in this form the being of general things participates on a continuing basis in that through it they are presented for the organic function in the being and becoming of subordinate individual things.

The commonality presented in judgment is one of two things. Either it is the commonality between beings of the same kind, and then action can be represented, on the one hand, as grounded in the two coefficients, in part as in the common nature of the two, in which the possibility both of doing and of undergoing lies. Or, on the other hand, it is the commonality of things that are not of the same kind. In the latter case, a single cause is to be found only in the higher concept involved, a concept to which the two spheres are subordinated. In this way, all that precedes it between two such spheres also permits of being viewed as the act of one higher and general being—but always as an act, thus under the form of judgment and in an indirect fashion—and all that precedes it is viewed as the act of absolute being, under which everything is included.

The Unity of the Formal and Transcendental in the Formation of Concepts and Judgments

Lecture 20

Thus, since knowing stands under the form of judgment, we must also posit with it a being that corresponds to the form of judgment. This means:

---

an object. The exact opposite obtains with "intransitive" (as in the verbs "exist," "live," "bloom").

47. *Historisches.*

1. In the sphere of individual things it is a being-in-common subordinate to their distinctive and particular being, one whereby they produce individual actions in common. This being-in-common is, first of all, that with things of the same kind, then that with others and essentially a totality so that the entire area is expressed in the states of the individual thing and the existence of that thing is contained in this expression of the entire area.

2. In the sphere of general things there is a breaking down into contrasts whereby both of the contrasted factors of the given action are grounded in one higher being.

3. Hence, in absolute being there is a breaking down into a totality of contrasts that take place from original life on, a process whereby all actions are referred back to this original life and are grounded in it, also whereby what is absolute and the total being-in-common of all individual things are one and the same.

What the two domains of concept and judgment are comprised of:

1. Formally, the two together are the entirety of knowing, and this entirety is thus always constructed through subsumption and combination. The system of concepts forms the steady scaffolding, while the system of judgments forms what fills it up in a vital fashion.

2. Transcendentally, the being of types and the being of actions comprise the totality of all being—all being exists in what is absolute.

Lecture 21

Note: Even judgments expressed through intransitive verbs are expressions of a being-in-common. The other [transitive] factor in action is situated in time, which in fact expresses the being-in-common of a given thing with all the rest.[48]

---

48. Ed. note: Twesten's notes captured the following explanation. "All transitive actions do in any case presuppose a commonality (*Gemeinschaft*), but it seems to be otherwise with intransitive actions. For example, 'The tree is blooming' seems simply to refer to something in the tree. However, transitive action is also contained in the concept as a possibility. That the tree blooms lies in its concept; that it is blooming now—the chronological reference contains something the basis of which is contained in something other than the tree. This feature can be applied to all cases; every activity thus has a twofold factor." Jonas's summary from a student transcript in SW III.4:2 (1839), p. 325, states: "That the tree is blooming now is grounded in its being-in-common (*Zusammensein*) with something other than the tree."

Addenda:

1. In every thing actions of all levels are present right up to the most general, so that the identity of the two factors lies only in what is absolute. Thus, the being of each individual thing contains all higher being in the totality of its actions, likewise in its concept, only in the first instance internally and in the second externally. The elapsing of being is a moving apart.

2. The whole being of an individual thing thus permits of being viewed as the being-in-common of all actions under the potency of its concept, just as the individual moment of a thing permits of being viewed as the being-in-common of all its being that persists under the potency of the predicate. So, here everything exists in each part.

3. One can already see from this situation how the subordination between what persists and what elapses is reciprocal, as is true of the subordination between being and doing, and each distinct subordination provides the ground for some onesidedness.

4. This subordination entirely disappears in the idea of the absolute, which is the pure identity of being and doing, and the same is true with respect to the persistence of concept and object.

Note: Both instances of identity may be posited only in one and the same entity. This is true in part because it is simply the same being that is identical with the two and in part because the formula by which we have arrived at them demands it, for concept and judgment may be based only on each other.

5. Every individual thing has its concept and therewith has the scale of persisting being entirely within itself; it has only a part in the concepts of its predicates.

Lecture 22
(Monday, June 24)

That is, the representation of a thing holds the concept of its kind entirely within itself, and this concept is also entirely the same in all representations of individual things; they are different not through this concept of kind but only through something else. The vital force in the thing is of course not entire, because it is only a part of its production. (From this point arises the issue raised in Plato's *Parmenides*.)[49]

6. If each action is constituted of two factors in this way, then the question concerning its cause viewed as singular is simply the question concerning the

---

49. Ed. note: This issue appears in Plato's dialogue, *Parmenides*, 130a–c.

other factor involved that is outside the thing to which a given change is attributed as subject. However, the nature of this thing is not to be posited as cause; rather, one must either stick with the given action itself or place the factor right into the *complexus* of all things. The cause or thing wherein the action is grounded is simply the higher unity, and the ultimate unity is the absolute. — More correct, therefore, is the old terminology to the effect that two things produce together. Gender is the vital scheme for division into factors.

7. If the syllogism were a distinct form of knowing, a distinct being would also have to correspond to it; however, it is not possible to demonstrate such a thing, for the fact that being and doing are not to be divorced from each other is already delineated in the way in which concept and judgment depend on each other. The contents of the syllogism consist only in the fact that if a lower feature is subsumed under a higher one, such actions as may be possible are also assumed with it. New cognition cannot possibly arise in this fashion. In its form the syllogism is a transition from one judgment through a concept to another judgment; it thus indicates the interlacing of the two trains of thought, each of which we already know even without this.[50]

---

50. Ed. commentary: It has already been indicated that in the processes of thinking that produce knowing judgments and concepts are interdependent. Now, judgments especially contrast with concepts as what is historical contrasts with what is philosophical, and the distinct validation thus appears in activity that is carried out in and through the mind's organic function as in the being and becoming of individual things. Whether on the side more of self-initiated action or on the side more of receptivity, with respect to knowing historical entities may appear as of the same kind or of different kinds but always as subordinate to some higher concept. (For example, Roman Catholic and Evangelical-Protestant institutions, with the faith and action respectively represented in them, belong under the more general concept of "Christian." The history of Christianity, however, is not left to drift on an empty plain. Ultimately, in the sense of origins as well as of eventual destinations, Christianity is to be seen as the act of absolute being, as are all other modes of faith in their histories.) Nothing in history is purely individual, for each individual action is in part an aspect or product of common action, and over time contrasts appear among actions and their consequents. (For example, doctrines concerning the triune God evolved in this way in the early centuries of the church. Schleiermacher wrote a long essay in 1822 to try to reconstruct the development of major contrasts and both their resolution and their continuing presence over the history of doctrine. This major essay has been included in Schleiermacher's *The Triune God*, a collection also including two sermons and chapters on the subject from his 1823 and 1831 *Christian Faith*, edited and translated by me and by Edwina Lawler.)

In terms of knowing, all these contrasting features that appear historically are to be viewed as successively subsumed under concepts, which are used like a "scaffolding" to grasp the meanings of what has been discriminated out by individual and shared judgments over time. These judgments, however, are what fills out the scaffolding; they are the elements of experience that make history a living thing. Moreover, taking the larger picture (the transcendental one), they as much as concepts comprise the totality of all being and becoming in history, both natural and human, for "all being exists in what is absolute."

With respect to human history, then—and there are parallels with respect to natural history and the ongoing work of the physical sciences, since they must be conducted by human

Lecture 23

Observations concerning what has been found thus far:

1. We have sought what is transcendental, hovering over what is real, and we have sought what is formal, in a distinction between knowing and thinking that is not assured though it has also referred to what is real. The transcendental refers to occasionally clearer construction of the physical and ethical domains as the relative identity of concept and object, in that in the physical domain what is

---

beings—Schleiermacher might well have said with a successor, R.G. Collingwood, that "all history is the history of thought," composed by the observing and reflecting mind of an interposing of judgments and concepts, of what is distinctive and what has more general meaning intertwined.

Apart from the ultimate absolute, causation within this stream of events is difficult to assign in a strict sense, for there is no clear way to cut through the overall process of history ("the *complexus* of all things") without cutting it short. Certainly, no deductive procedure would in itself even approximate an adequate historical account, for the premises in a genuine deductive argument are already supposed to contain anything that the conclusion might arrive at, and the problems of thinking historically are precisely those of finding all the relevant proximate causes and of uncovering their real interactions.

So, if this mode of reconstruction is warranted, as it seems to be, what Schleiermacher is giving us in his account of judgment is a very guarded philosophy of history, both human and natural in form, written with the broadest possible scope. At the same time, it is a markedly positive philosophy of history in that, insofar as history is rethought and recorded (not just chronicled), it is "positive" in two senses. First, given adequate information, it can reasonably be expected to have positive and not negative or seriously hampered results, for it is a history of being. Second, it reflects the discriminations, decisions and corresponding actions of social, not just individual, entities, so that what is presented can be validated in social terms; it can, as it were, carry its own consensual validation and is open to public scrutiny. One of Schleiermacher's own predilections was to look very closely at creative, "original" ideas and their corresponding events, so as to have a base from which to observe continuities and changes over time. This is quite consistent with his attention to beginnings here, as well as to ongoing, changing intentions as historical processes continue along recognizable, reconstructable lines.

See Schleiermacher's works in "ethics," conceived as "the science of the principles of [human] history (*Geschichte*)," for details as to how he would have inquiry organized and conducted in this general domain. There the entire array of sciences is seen to comprise a major domain in societies, alongside the family, church, state and what he calls "free sociality." Thus, while he nowhere attempts to give so full an account of the work of the physical sciences as he did of the human-social sciences, he does show some ways in which the two largest aspects of science interrelate. Such work is meant to fill in what is to be mapped out more generally in dialectic.

In the next lecture hour Schleiermacher sums up this historical process by reminding his listeners that what he calls "the absolute" is conceptually a terminus of it all, at every beginning and at the very end, thus is present also throughout, wherever thinking that is knowing is done—if only incompletely. This is another, indirect, way of showing that the transcendental and the formal—the metaphysical and the logical, technical—aspects of thinking form a unity.

objective is original and reason is what is being built upon it and in the ethical domain reason is original and the object is what is being built upon it. We have sought the two as one and have found it to be such in the absolute.

2. One can indeed say that the transcendent is the absolute itself, and the formal is the concept of the absolute. However, we deny the difference, for as we sought the formal we found being along with it, and as we sought the transcendental we found the concept along with it. Two things are involved here: (a) that to the extent that the concept of the absolute exists in us, the absolute itself also exists in us—we have the concept of the absolute not as this or that individual thing but have it as reason, and as such we have also approached what is supreme as closely as possible; (b) that insofar as we are not the absolute itself, we also do not have the concept of the absolute—thus, we do not have it from the side of organic function but only as the formal element common to all acts of cognition, and its organic side would exist only in the totality of all knowledge of what is finite and individual. Thus, we are involved in forming a vital perspective on the deity to the extent that we work on the completion of the real sciences. This happens, however, not when a detail is added to other details merely as an aggregate but only through systematic treatment in which the totality of all this is at least striven for.[51]

3. Except to assert that the deity as transcendent being is the principle of all being and as transcendent idea is the formal principle of all knowing, nothing more is to be said of it in the domain of knowing. All else is simply bombast or an admixing of the religious, which is out of bounds here and can actually have only a corruptive effect if placed within the bounds.[52]

---

51. Ed. note: Schleiermacher's seminal 1808 essay presenting *Occasional Thoughts on Universities in the German Sense*, tr. by myself and Edwina Lawler (Lewiston, N.Y.: Edwin Mellen Press, 1991) includes an overview of desirable relationships among the sciences but without much reference to the deity. This and other related documents by Schleiermacher are included in the larger volume (same translators), *Writings on Academia* (same press, forthcoming), with editorial essays placing his views in historical context.

52. Ed. note: See my volume containing all three editions (1799, 1806, 1821) of *On Religion* (Lewiston, N.Y.: Edwin Mellen Press, 1996) for his fullest accounts of this matter, also offered in somewhat greater detail in later sections here (especially the hour following; see also index) and in later sets of lectures on dialectic. See also *Christian Faith* on relations between God and world in a Christian perspective.

The Absolute with Respect to
God and World

Lecture 24

Comparison of our view of the deity with other views:

Since we posit the absolute as the fundament of all thinking, we have to assume that the idea of deity is present in everything; but in this way we are in dispute with those who separate God from the world.

1. Suppose that the world is posited as eternal without God. In this case (a) not all that is would be in mind, for if one takes all that is as implicit in reason, one arrives at an absolute reason; (b) that which is would not be as it is thought to be, because individual being would not be contained in the concept unless one claimed that what is thought of is an inner being, for in this way one arrives at an absolute being; (c) this position provides no warranty whatsoever for a correspondence between being and thinking; its surety rests on opinion alone.

2. Suppose that the world is posited as temporal through God, thus that the absolute is sheer thinking, namely thinking regarding the world. Now, if nothing is added with respect to God through that being of the world, which comes into being later, it is also not grounded in God. If something is added, then a difference actually exists in God between what is essential and what is accidental. Hence, in this regard this point also remains irresolvable.

The first argument agrees with our view in that God is not to be separated from the world and the second argument agrees with our view in that reason is original. These two points, however, do not arrive at any pure identity of concept and object.

3. Suppose that God and matter were both eternal, while the interlocking of the two is temporal; that would yield an original duality, and both aspects of the absolute would be mythical.)

Now, since we derive the correspondence between thinking and being in real knowing only from the original identity of the two in the absolute, one must apply both views to reach a different explanation. Also in what is real, thinking and being appear to us to be the same overall as interlocking and being-in-common only in their dependence on a single higher being and thinking. Here thinking and being must appear as subordinate, in accordance with the form of causality.

Thus, a first option would be that thinking is viewed as the effect of being. In this case, being is simply matter. (The mythical content of this concept is such that thinking viewed as a particular action of matter—materialism—cannot any longer provide a complete mirroring of it.)[53]

Lecture 25
(Monday, July 1)

Repetition and extension of the previous hour:

We have arrived at the point of showing that the idea of the absolute (also apart from its religious form) is present everywhere in thinking and in part laid out under an incomplete form, in part insofar as it is itself incomplete, renders the comprehension of knowing difficult.

Suppose an intelligent God with an arbitrary world, and over against that God an eternal chaos with arbitrary or incomprehensible formation of the world out of that. Here the idea of the absolute is present in form, because something original is set forth as the ground of what is finite, but as to matter it is set forth onesidedly and as something placed in opposition to matter. The relationship of the absolute to the world remains unclear. Knowing must be explained insufficiently, based on causality.

Suppose that God and chaos exist alongside each other and there are only arbitrary, secondary interventions of God upon chaos, also that over against this is an eternal world without God and without chaos. Materially speaking, the idea of the absolute is present, but not in form for this idea does not have primacy. In the first statement the idea of God is not the principle; rather, one is driven beyond it to dualism. In the second statement the idea of God is not thought of in itself at all; rather, it is thought of only in the totality of what is relative, something that is of itself inconceivable.

In materialism thinking is posited as effect or a phenomenon of matter. The truth therein is referred to the side of organic function, while the formal function is missing entirely. The unconscious idea of the absolute resists the subordination of thinking to matter, with the result that among many a theistic materialism is formed; that is, the sum total of matter stands in turn under a higher thinking, and so the idea of the absolute is constituted in a secondary way and as an inconsistency.

In spiritualism—whether Leibnizian or Fichtian[54]—matter is viewed as a phenomenon of spirit. The unconscious idea of the absolute resists that too, and

---

53. Ed. note: The second option is identified with a contrasting "spiritualism" in the next lecture hour.

54. Ed. note: Arndt (p. 98) has found and quotes the pertinent references from Leibniz in his letter to Bernoulli of August 22, 1698, to which Schleiermacher refers in his earlier Leibniz

in that actual existence[55] is denied, a higher, absolute being is posited to exist above the I. If this is to be anything, it must be the true idea of the absolute, but then the denial of actual existence also comes to a halt. Here the truth refers to the formal function, but the organic function is not to be comprehended, thus the idea of knowing is also destroyed.

This is the indirect proof of our original claim that the transcendental and formal are a unity.

Lecture 26

What has been said is not supposed to be a complete polemic. Rather, it is supposed to show how the other views stand in comparison with ours, especially in relation to the explanation of knowing.

Our view rests on the fact that the correspondence of thinking and being that resides in the idea of knowing is derived from the original identity of the two in the absolute.

This is also still evident when one observes thinking as action. Thereby an immediate unity of the object and the concept, which are otherwise separate, is posited, and this action is to be understood only on the basis of the higher sphere in which the two factors are one, namely on the basis of the absolute.

In every notion the concept produces the formal element in us and the object outside us produces the organic element, which to begin with contains only something arbitrary with respect to that concept. Then, what is in the two is so assuredly the same as what is in the absolute, only in the one in an ideal fashion and in the other in a real fashion, that the two exactly coincide also in action, which is intelligible through the absolute alone.[56]

notes in KGA I.2 (1984), pp. 85 and 93. Arndt aptly explains: "As force, matter is for Leibniz a representation of the monad and is in this sense interpretable as 'appearance of mind'." For Fichte, whom Arndt also quotes, he explains: "The usual representation of matter is a product of the empirical I." See Fichte's *Versuch einer neuen Darstellung der Wissenschaftslehre.* Erste Abteilung, 5. Abschnitt (1797)—in the Academie Ausgabe 1,4, 191ff; also in his Zweite Einleitung to this work, 6. Abschnitt—in the same edition, 1,4, 243.

55. *Dasein.*

56. Ed. commentary: Here, as throughout, the absolute is the idea that represents what is whole and transcendental in all thinking that bears the status of knowing. Here he is also returning to the analysis of sentences, wherein we put forth a concept, which is a formal element that in the action that is thinking is directed to an object, the organic element. These two elements are posited as one in the absolute. That is to say, there is some overall, total meaning of which the sentence with its various elements is a part, and this is taken to inform the sentence insofar as it is an instance of knowing. Even though the universe is constantly in process, we are, unstatically, a part of that whole of being. Even if thoughts and events were conceived as always being to some extent unpredictable, containing some arbitrariness and newness in them, they are not for that reason wholly isolated and disconnected from the rest.

In this fashion knowing is conceivable. However, the just as actual non-knowing, error, must also be comprehended in just this way. This can genuinely happen only once the formal side of the entire presentation comes out more.

In a preliminary way, we may simply say the following. Since in our action of thinking the concept also exists in some entity, which at the same time takes part in the nature of what is objective, and since in every action each entity that is acting does so completely, so, whatever extraneous feature is taken in must disturb cognition, unless with respect to cognition the action is cleanly set apart.

Lecture 27

Addendum and transition to the formal part:

If we now proceed to construct real information, we are thus in the domain of real knowing, thus of the ethical and the physical. Still, the two areas cannot be derived there, because one would be abstracting from their difference from each other and that derivation must be accomplished in the general work of philosophy. Thus, we must have that derivation in some fashion already without knowing it.

If one applies the contrast between concept and object to being, the separation cannot be an absolute one but can be a relative one, because otherwise the two would be posited entirely on the basis of what is absolute. Thus, being in which concept comes to the fore is ideal being, and being in which the object comes to the fore is real being (to posit the two as totally separate, as pure spirit and pure matter, is simply mythical). The two are bound to a subordinate, secondary unity in the idea of the world; the two placed in contrast to each other as physical and ethical knowing are bound into one in the idea of science.

The idea of the world can be conceived as a unity pure and simple,[57] but also as a totality made up of a plurality of specially relativized unities. Both conceptions are true; the latter unities in totality are givens, the former is what is necessary to think of.

Every one is nested, as it were, and from there extends out to the whole as are birds in flight. Schleiermacher's own, more orderly images here remain those of the scale or ladder of forms presenting being (not a chair or a clear-fixed system and not a two-leveled being) and of the building with its scaffolding and contents, but these must also be imagined as extending out to the whole.

57. *Als Einheit schlechthin.*

So, the idea of the world also determines the boundaries of our knowing. We are bound to the earth.[58] All operations of thinking, even the entire system of our concept forming must be grounded therein.

Lecture 28
(Monday, July 8)

Continuation:

The idea of the world was not meant to be an actual derivation from the absolute but was only meant to express the relationship between the two to the extent that they are different and to the extent that they are the same. The notion that finite being is a fall from God[59] is full of absurdity and contradiction, since the same relationship of the two with respect to each other prevails always and eternally.

Regarding the idea of the world, in our account we always have only the formal element, which essentially proceeds from the process of deduction. What is real must likewise essentially proceed from the process of induction, and this can only gradually come to completion. Thus, the two do not occur simultaneously, so that on this account too a noncoincidence of the two exists and thus error is possible.

Every instance of real knowing must refer to some element of the world, thus to a being in which there is also in turn an identity of concept and object. From the perspective of being that reasons, the concept seems to be a diminishing factor but never vanishing entirely. What appears to us to be dead here must simply be taken up into a higher sphere and thus cannot be imagined of itself.

Just as the absolute stands under the form of identity, which form, however, grasps the fullness of contrasts under itself and in itself, accordingly the world and all that is in it stands under the form of contrast. Thus, the first, negative canon of the procedure is that no contrast is absolute; rather, all contrasts are

---

58. Ed. commentary: This does not mean, of course, that the objects of our observation are restricted to earth. Schleiermacher took the *Universum* to be much larger than that. In his time, however, he would have had to think that even the observations of astronomers were earth-bound. Nonetheless, even today we are people of the earth, and wherever we may eventually roam it may be reasonably supposed that we will be so in large part, carrying our physical and human "world" with us.

59. Arndt note (p. 98f): "On the conception that finite being is a fall from God compare F.W.J. Schelling, *Philosophie und Religion* (1804), in *Sämmtliche Werke* I.6 (Stuttgart/Augsburg, 1860), p. 38: 'The Absolute is the only entity that is real. In contrast, finite things are not real. Hence, their basis cannot lie in an impartation of reality to them or to their substratum, which would be an impartation from the Absolute but can lie only in a distancing, in a fall from the Absolute'."

only relative. An instance of thinking that isolates a supposedly absolute contrast represents nothing actual.[60]

Since collectively investigations concerning form refer to real knowing, one must simply look to the being-in-common of that which predominately comes to the fore out of the process of induction. The latter (the result of organic function) proceeds from the representing of what is individual and particular. This is in every case a quantum and stands under the conditions of time and space. Something must therefore be said about this subject.[61]

---

60. Ed. note: This is why *Gegensatz*, a technical term often mistakenly referred to in the literature as if it necessarily meant "opposite," or "polar opposite" or "antithesis," is almost always to be translated "contrast" in Schleiermacher's discourse. There is nothing in his meaning of "contrast," moreover, that requires contrasts always to come in twos, though in practice he does show a bias toward twos. Such a bias immediately derives from predominant though not exclusive structures in German, as in a great many other languages. Alternative depictions of contrasts do appear in Schleiermacher's discourse, however, and are perhaps even more to be recommended.

61. Ed. commentary: This excursus regarding space and time is intended further to show in what ways we are bound to the earth and thus to its principal conditions of space and time. This is true, he says, even with respect to our general concepts. Then, the brief excursus relating to what students of that period could find out about common logic from Baumgarten's notable textbook makes a further transition via a critique of false claims frequently made for common logic. This critique indicates that a major reason for lecturing about the formal, or technical, aspect of dialectic lies in what he rightly takes to be the extremely damaging effects on science of building systems of thought through logical contrivances. Schleiermacher wants to insist on holding a tie to what is real in the forming and combining of both concepts and judgments in all the sciences.

Except in the expansion of its appended "inductive," "heuristic" and "architectonic" uses, common, demonstrative or deductive (Aristotelian) logic—as it is variously called—has not greatly changed in form since Schleiermacher's time. A century later, in a great work entitled *Principia Mathematica*, Alfred North Whitehead and Bertrand Russell showed that mathematics itself has its roots in symbolic logic, an outgrowth of deductive logic that had begun to flourish late in the previous century. Schleiermacher had developed a love of mathematics in school, and its terms are to be found throughout his writings. The question arises: Is his critique likely to touch the now obviously valuable use of mathematics in the natural sciences? To the degree that hypotheses thus derived are considered to be truth rather than provisional statements making truth claims and are used to form elaborate theoretical systems that remain untested, probably yes. Otherwise not. As he states in the 29th lecture, "all real knowing is at the same time something quantitative." Since such knowing, to which all science aspires, has quantitative elements, and since he recognizes a "need to set hypotheses" (in the 48th lecture), there seems to be no reason consistent with his view for rejecting the sophisticated mathematical methods used in natural science or, where applicable, in other sciences.

What Schleiermacher had strong grounds for opposing in his own time was an excessive use of deduction for system building, not only in philosophy but in science as well. He saw this habit to be seriously hampering of the progress of science and, in effect, a sheer work of fantasy. In the opposite direction, the then current habits of many empiricists he saw to be equally damaging, for in their reliance on so-called "data" they tended to be unaware of the limiting nature of their judgments and wrongly eschewed discovery of the intricate interconnections among the phenomena they were investigating. Although some had indeed

Space and Time

First of all, in a negative sense we must not say that only the notions of individuals stand under these conditions, for even what is most general takes part in organic function. We must also not say that the two refer only to our senses, for the results of organic function are results of its being-in-common with things.

Lecture 29

Continuation regarding time and space:

General things also stand under the form of space. The way in which living forces are spread over the earth and the measure in which they produce individual entities comprise spacial relations. — They have temporal relations in the same way. In time there are dissimilarities of productive power and dissimilar relationships among its various functions.

Space and time comprise the way in which things themselves exist—not only our notions—which results from our main view concerning knowing, because all real knowing is at the same time something quantitative. Thus, both forms are present in notions as well as in things, and the question as to which of the two they are is vacuous.

---

gotten beyond the vulgar trial-and-error empiricism of Roger Bacon (ca 1220-1292), they did not yet show themselves to be adept at the concept-forming and integrating activity also necessary to science. The embattled factors, under the heads of "induction," "deduction" and "combination," are what the second, formal part is all about.

Even before I had gained a more nearly full-fledged understanding of what Schleiermacher was trying to accomplish in his presentation of dialectic, I was able to discern his remarkably full and prescient understanding of science—virtually unequalled in his century and rarely grasped in our own—simply through an intimate knowledge of how he himself went to work. Only a portion of this understanding can be gleaned from the lectures on dialectic in any case, for, unlike Fichte, he did not purport to offer a complete "theory of science" there. His more modest effort was that of clearing the way for such theory. See my essay "Schleiermacher on the Scientific Study of Religion," in Herbert Richardson, ed., *Friedrich Schleiermacher and the Founding of the University of Berlin: The Study of Religion as a Scientific Discipline* (Lewiston, N.Y.: Edwin Mellen Press, 1991), 45-82. The fullest formal, general account of the organization and procedures of a single science, in keeping with his university appointment, was of the "positive science" theology. This field, he indicated, has real objects like any other (the highest being conveyed in communion of the faithful with God) but is aimed at a social purpose, as law and medicine are—in this case, leadership of the Christian church. See *Brief Outline of Theology as a Field of Study* (Lewiston, N.Y.: Edwin Mellen Press, 1990).

The question as to whether space is something of itself always rests, if only as yet concealed, on the notion of empty space. However, there is no such thing. Even if it is not filled with matter, it is filled with action.

Everything that stands under the form of contrast also stands under these two forms, time and space. They are posited simultaneously with divided and relative being. Space is the outside-each-other of being, time the outside-each-other of doing. Inner space or filled space represents the manifold of a thing in the unity of its being. Every filled space represents an inner contrast; where this contrast ceases, as does that between soul and body, there is also no spacial relation there.[62] Every intermediate space represents an external contrast; where this contrast ceases, as occurs with the world overall, there is also no intermediate space there. Action negates space. Two agents are immediately present to each other. The external contrast of an action, whereby it is distinguished from another action, is designated by the term filled time; its internal contrast, whereby it is divided within itself into action and reaction, is designated by the term intermediate time.

This perspective on the meaning of time and space belongs only in this place. All further meaning would be lodged either in physics or in mathematics.

A Critique of Common Logic

Lecture 30

On common logic, with regard especially to that of A.G. Baumgarten:[63]

Our task of constructing thinking each time so that it will become an instance of knowing, and of knowing each time how closely a given instance of thinking approaches the idea of knowing, was supposed to have been fulfilled up to now by logic. Hence the need to ponder the insufficiency of logic once more.

Besides the three elementary chapters of logic, which do not suffice because they provide no rule for making advances in thinking, heuristic also comes into consideration, and heuristic is divided into two parts, empirical and a priori. In isolation, however, they do not permit of finding anything. Moreover, the a priori part refers back to the other part, because its axioms are based on definitions.

---

62. Ed. note: See Schleiermacher's lectures on psychology (SW III.6, 1862) for a full elucidation of this and related points.

63. Arndt (p. 99) cites related passages in Alexander Gottlieb Baumgarten's *Acroasis Logica in Christianum L.B. de Wolff* (Halle, 1761). There conclusions in the syllogism are treated with concepts and judgments as the three elements of logic. Schleiermacher excludes conclusions (see the 10th lecture).

The definition is the salient point, because it forms the transition between the concept formation and sentence formation. It is a major error to suppose that real definition and nominal definition are members of a kind, since only the real definition constructs an instance of knowing as an element of science, while the nominal definition constructs something arbitrary and fragmentary. This comparison shows that logic does not proceed to construction of knowing but only to what is fragmentary. A second major error is to suppose that logic in accordance with its form places all value on the formation of sentences, with which heuristic is exclusively occupied; all sentence formation, however, rests on axioms, and these are formed by means of identical sentences from definitions. Thus, all contrivance in this area is fixed on definitions and as a result on concept formation, to which logic offers practically no entry.

The history of science confirms how bad the situation has been up to now with respect to concept formation, since the field of observation is indeed always broadening but systems follow upon each other with ever greater speed. Our entire period, right down to the few points where the deficiency of logic has been felt, bears within it the character of Aristotle as its founder.

II. THE FORMAL, OR TECHNICAL,[64] PART

Lecture 31
(Monday, July 15)

Introduction to Part Two:

Now, we have to apply what we have found up to this point (1) to formation of concepts and (2) to formation of judgments. Note: In logic it has been a defect to offer no rules for transition beyond the useless syllogism, because there the intention is to force everything into the deductive structure. We have no formal principle other than the perception of knowing itself, and every particular is true for us to the extent that it bears this perception in itself. Previously we have moved from that perception upward to the absolute, and now we move downward to the particular. Concerning the joining of the two we can speak only in an appendix.[65]

Before we get into classification, there is still something in common to the two forms that rests on the perception of knowing as something that is coming into being; this perception we have to pursue further here.

What is thinking when it is not an instance of complete knowing?

---

64. Ed. note: Already in 1814/15, Schleiermacher was using both "formal" and "technical" for this second part and did so thereafter.

65. Schleiermacher: "Further note: A systematic treatment would surely consist of the combination of what is found through construction. Essentially, this process is, to be sure, one of subsumption. — Then even construction is itself combination and can be treated in terms of the question as to which contrasts intersect and assume each other." — Ed. note: Already in the 1814/15 lectures Schleiermacher further divides the section on "combination" into two sub-sections on "heuristic procedures" and "architectonic procedures." This organization is briefly suggested in the 1811 notes and was followed in the more detailed presentations from 1814/15 on. An excellent example of what he was pointing to in the above note is found in the organization of his *Christian Faith*. As elsewhere here, "perception" is used as distinuished from "sense perception." See note 28.

Either such an act of thinking lacks the character of knowing with consciousness, and then, if the thinker is taking an objective direction, it is an incomplete act, a not-yet-knowing, but if it is complete the thinker is taking no objective direction and the act of thinking is pure fantasy. Or the character of knowing is lacking in the act of thinking without consciousness, and then it is an error. Or the act of thinking has the character of knowing without consciousness and then it is a correct opinion, in which both have instinctively coincided without perception of the whole in the particular.

Thus, in that we are proceeding upon the construction of error, we must learn how to test whether we continually have the absolute in the particular and how we have to protect ourselves against error during the whole course of thinking.

Thus, we must learn to understand error first of all in general terms.

A new confusion of the principle of distinctiveness, which confusion occurs in fantasizing: a point of departure is posited with the quality of individual necessity, but this should be referred back to what is general in nature.

Lecture 32

The two functions of thinking must be posited as independent from each other. It is not that the originally single act of thinking initially divides itself into the two aspects but that every individual act of thinking is simply a uniting of the two. Each function is perpetually in an all around activity; the individual act of thinking simply arises out of this activity and originates from this two-sided arising. We always have far more in mind than we perceive and also have far more in our reason than is formed into concepts by us.

Thereby the error is possible of supposing that no necessary tie between the two sorts of element exists within us. At the instant of union there is no guarantee that the two functions of thinking will belong together. This guarantee is first formed from the entire system of knowing, and in this way one can say that knowing originates from error.

The original form of judgment is the establishment of a concept out of an individual action (and is the reverse true?).[66]

---

66. Ed. commentary: Earlier discussions here, together with what Schleiermacher has just said in this introduction to the second part about the complex, "all around activity" of our minds, suggest that in practice this is a chicken-and-egg question. In the next hour, the question is immediately reframed.

Lecture 33

The question arises as to which of the two functions of thinking we should take up first, concept or judgment?

Proceeding historically, we would have to take judgment first, because obviously actions rather than things are posited in the consciousness of children.[67] When a child sets itself over against things it must at the same time posit itself as something individual, but what is individual first comes forth, gradually, from what is universal, which must thus precede it. — Language also confirms this. The impersonal verb was, of course, earlier than the personal verb, which presupposes a concept as subject. The grammatical dignity of the third person in Hebrew usage indicates that it was originally the impersonal verb, to which the sense of personal existence was then added,[68] and we too still use the impersonal verb to the degree that objects are not completely separate for us. Hence, it is also a very salutary process wherever the constitution of an instance of real knowing comes up to set aside the existing formation of a concept and to view everything independently from the viewpoint of action.

Here, however, where we are concerned more with the construction of something formal, the other view must precede, the view that in its complete form judgment presents a synthesis that arises from concepts, so that concept must precede judgment as the elementary form.

Introduction to the formation of concepts:

The verb represents a concept just as much as the substantive noun does; it is action placed under the potency of concept. This is so, for the verb has the same identity of general and particular in it that constitutes the nature of any concept; the individual action is also simply an expression of a more widely extended general function. Thus, there are two classes of concepts: those that by their nature are subjects and can become predicates only in an indirect fashion and

---

67. Ed. commentary: For example, "Michael went down the slide" is the report of an action, which can then be posited as a thing to think about. If Michael is an infant, he would have perceived differences among shapes or colors, which entails making a perceptual discrimination not immediately dependent on a concept; but being able to discern, in a judgment that belongs to thinking, that red objects share the quality of being red is a next step, and this involves having a concept, albeit an inchoate one. It is highly likely, moreover, that people originally thought in terms of sentences like "this is done" or "one does this," as he goes on to suggest, and that it was only with introduction of further elements, notably an identification of "I" and "me" and "us" and "that other," that consciousness arose much beyond the sense perceptual level of mentation.

68. Arndt note: "In Hebrew usage the pattern of conjugation begins with the third, not the first person."

those that by their nature are predicates and can becomes subjects only indirectly.[69]

In general terms, it applies to both classes of concepts that no concept formation is ever complete, right up to the point of completed knowing, precisely on account of the identity of the general and the particular. Every concept that stands under the absolute has, at the same time, a type of particularity, because it does not emerge from construction as the only thing that is real. Now, the particular is that which is purely given in being but is not purely contained in thinking, and the general is that which is completely given in thinking but is not to be exhibited purely in being. Thus, the two are asymptotes, and only in relation to the absolute as a necessary supplement can their identity be completed. It is therefore necessary to know wherefrom every element of a concept stems and increasingly to build the two kinds of subjects into each other. Only in this way will we be able to distinguish what among our concepts is knowing and what is not knowing.

The Formation of Concepts

Lecture 34
(Monday, July 22)

Characterization of the two classes of concept:

1. With concepts that express action the quantitative feature comes to the fore; they are concepts of which Plato says that they admit of a more or less.[70] (In the substantive form this is no longer so recognizable as in the pure verb. It is

---

69. Ed. commentary: Most obviously, "Katherine," as a proper name, can become a predicate only indirectly, as in the sentence "The girl in the blue dress running over there is Katherine," while "blue" is naturally a predicate and can become a subject only indirectly (by inversion) as in "Blue is the color of my true love's eyes" or as in a disquisition on the concept "blue" (William Gass wrote such a thing). Also, in a sentence such as "The absolute is the identity of concept and judgment, being and thinking, subject and object," the subject is ultimately taken to be indeterminate and by definition not strictly a subject or a predicate, except in the most formal-grammatical sense.

70. Arndt note: "Regarding this 'more and less' in Plato's thought, Twesten's note reads: 'Particular activities can scarcely be designated other than quantitatively, by a more or less. For example, in love there is a more or less at the same time; an action of this kind does not come to consciousness otherwise than with intention. (See Plato's *Parmenides* and *Charmides*, where the discussion is about whether there are ideas where there is a more or less. Productive power in its identity with concept constitutes the idea.)' Cf. Plato, *Parmenides* 149d–151e, *Charmides* 168b–169c."

least recognizable in the relative adjectives and substantives that Plato cites: small and large, smallness and largeness; nevertheless, it is easily shown that these too are actions.) With the direct substantives the quantitative feature recedes, and what is self-determined and has no capacity for degrees comes to the fore. An instance of love, for example, is moreso than some other, while a horse is no more a horse than any other even if it is bigger.

2. With concepts that represent a being the process of subordination goes through a feature of distinct plurality through many stages up to the individual; in these stages, which express action, subordination recedes and coordination under the form of indistinct plurality comes to the fore. The first process is natural, since every being is a derived unity that in turn divides into a distinct circle of contrasts. The second process is natural, since every action is a being-in-common of a function of the subject with some other object and not every such being-in-common can form a particular kind.

Lecture 35

Addendum to this characterization:

To point 1: The contrast indicated here is only a relative one. In reaching the terminus on the side of being, where the indistinct plurality mentioned enters in, one can no longer understand the individual in itself as necessary and distinct; rather, the difference between the one and the other emerges here only as a condition of productive power determined by time and locality, and this difference limits these as action and as more and less. Only with respect to human beings does one form the pretension of individuality that the individual is to be a thoroughgoing and subordinately analogous modification of the idea of the human being.

The same is true, however, on the side of action, when one regards action quite apart from all more narrow distinctness in a subject so that it appears as a necessary function, and with this view the more and less also vanish. (Every individual action still bears the more and less, because it has its crescendo and decrescendo. The same thing, however, also takes place with every individual thing only less affecting of its nature, thus also from this aspect relatively.)

To point 2: This contrast too is a relative one. The transition between the types of distinct and indistinct plurality occurs on the side of being through the middle concept of variety, which has something of each and in which the contrast is therefore lifted. In contrast, at the incomplete stages of being even the formation of a type is confused and appears to be a gradual transition (since the actual distinction indeed consists in the fact that even if kinds form a series none of them is actually to be viewed as a transition to another one).

Inferences: There thus follow two canons. (1) To regard something under the viewpoint of more and less and to regard it as action is one and the same thing. Accordingly, moreover, its being is fixed. (2) What can be regarded only under the form of indistinct plurality and thus is not to be typologized is to be regarded as action. Likewise, moreover, what can be subsumed under a distinct plurality must also be valid as a fixed being. This is an indication of results that flow herefrom for treatment of the sciences.

Induction

Lecture 36

Concept formation through induction:

Manifestly, induction emerges earlier than concept formation. Once construction becomes conscious, everything is found already to have been done through concept formation.

However, the two operations are never fully separated. Just as every instance of knowing a concept is an identity of the two, so too every operation in every moment of its activity is engaged in becoming one with the other operation.[71]

---

71. Ed. commentary: This account of induction over the next eight lectures, though brief, is more complex than the usual account. Moreover, it counters the simplistic distinction, frequently made right through the twentieth century, that induction ascends from the particular to the general whereas deduction descends from the general to the particular. At the outset of his discussion (in lectures 36–38), Schleiermacher divides induction into two moments, or operations, and a great many essential features are eventually attached to each, some of them familiar from other accounts but differently embedded. The two moments are deemed never to be fully separated from each other.

The first moment is identified chiefly from the viewpoint of individual empirical consciousness but even then in some fashion striving toward communication. Its task is to separate out items, or objects and actions, from the general field of experience. In some instances this is even done unconsciously and without the aid of any rules, as is true of infants sensing color and movement (for example, in the mother's face) or of adults when "faced with strange objects or too wide a field of vision." Even among infants (within a normal range of capacity), it will not be long before the second moment, or operation, of induction emerges and is joined to the first. Here the item, or object, of sense-oriented experience is "modeled after a member in the system of concepts" (which is likely to have been communicated to the infant through language or could conceivably have been formulated by the infant alone).

What is the nature of this "system"? (This term suggests that some interconnections have already been formed, often loosely termed "associations of ideas" in empirical psychology, but I do not recall Schleiermacher's ever using the German equivalent *Gedankenverbindung*,

Induction divides into two moments. The first moment is a separating of an object as a unity from the general mass. This can rest only on an action to which a part of the general mass is joined. The earliest indicators are color and movement, whereof one of these indicators is always the guarantee of the other. As is the case among children, so too among us when we are faced with strange objects or too wide a field of vision. Here no rule is actually available: everything is unconscious. An object will be correctly formed when it copies a member in the system of concepts. This system is innate—that is, it indwells us as an activity for the sake of an object to consciousness by means of its unity with the real side. The way in which an initial concurrence of this sort comes up can be called "memory."

A concept is formed only once the second moment is also present. A preliminary question arises as to which of the two moments has to do with error. It is true that what is sense-oriented is in itself just as little deluded as is reason in itself, but this recognition in itself is never an empirical point. Error lies in the being-in-common of the two, and every empirical point is such. Hence, error is possible in each of these two moments and also already in the preliminary positing of an object. People's tendency is to make their unity too great or too small. Thus, that unity is to be posited only provisionally.

Lecture 37
(Monday, July 29)

Just as individual being is extracted from the confused mass, so individual action is extracted from the confused general life.

Just as the positing of a thing rests on the perceiving of an action, so the positing of an action rests on the perceiving of a thing, with the result that the two

---

which would be off the mark for him.) It is "indwelling" or "innate," but only in the sense that it is first lodged unconsciously within us before it is brought to consciousness by a process called "memory."

In each of these operations some error is to be expected, as in the joining of the two. There is no automatic guarantee that what comes to consciousness through memory will be aptly connected to what is real or that its conceptual connections will be correct. (In short, there are no pure data, though some may come to be relied on for good reason. At best, data are "raw," but they are so not simply because they have not yet been "worked up," as is often claimed, but because of their very nature. We approach them cautiously, with well worked-out rules of procedure, then we do the best with them that we can, reexamining them and testing them in an unending cycle of inquiry.) — Note: These parenthetical remarks come more from a knowledge of other texts from Schleiermacher, which enable their use as interpretive implications drawn from the present text.

Schleiermacher thus devotes a considerable portion of his account to the nature of error and the ability to sort out error from what is true, a task never to be fully accomplished until the point of the absolute shall have been reached.

arise at the same time and through each other. Furthermore, the positing of action rests on two factors: space is represented and the result is represented. The same is true of the positing of a thing, only in a relationship that is reversed.

Just as in all these positings there is a confused mass that diminishes into something small or expands into something great, so with respect to what is comparatively great or small there is a general life from which individual actions are first to be separated out, so that the process goes ever onward.

Error can consist only in the object's being too great or too small for the action presupposed or the action's being too great or too small for the presupposed object. Since the process of the first instance is a preliminary one, so nothing is present there by which it could be justified. This can happen only through its own continuation, and the only criterion that emerges from this is that of positing what is thus posited only provisionally until such time as it has been verified in every respect as a unity[72] of the object or of the action.

If truth is present in such a moment, an identity of being and doing is thus present in it (since neither comes into being except through the other). An identity of induction and construction is also present, because this unity exists in contrast to the totality of the mass, thus has the form of contrast within itself.

The transition from the first into the second moment presupposes the plurality of the first. However, we can also think of the operation of the first moment only as a plurality that occurs at the same time.

Lecture 38

Continuation of the discussion on induction:

The first moment of induction is considered more from the viewpoint of individual empirical consciousness. However, since thinking intends also to be knowing, it also intends to become something identical that is present in many. Hence, even the first moment strives toward communication. True unity, however, is not yet found there; rather, what is found is being and doing that rest on each other, wherein each instance of being and doing rests in turn on a twofold sense perception. Hence, a multiplicity of features is further increased through the continuing observation of what has been posited in a number of points of time. This multiplicity, however, can appear only as an aggregate. It

---

72. *Einheit.* Ed. commentary: Here and in the next paragraph "unity" refers to the result of bringing all the relevant parts or features together into a true, integrated whole. As is explained, the object or action or other result (e.g. a concept) seen as a unity may still be involved in a contrast, hence not be wholly isolable from that contrast (e.g. with the totality of the mass to which it refers but with which it is by definition not identifiable).

does come to be a nominal definition,[73] the need for which is accounted for in terms of this multiplicity, but which also explains how it is for it to be able to emerge as a species alongside what is real instead of as preparatory to this.

If we consider the second moment of induction in large terms, based, first of all, on the viewpoint of the identity of knowing in everyone, what has come into being historically may seem thoroughly contradictory to this feature. Strictly taken, the vocabulary of one language obviously never corresponds to that of another, not at least in many regions. Likewise, over time concepts in the region of one and the same language are altered, so that one word ranges over a series of meanings.

At first, the coexisting difference here is not error but is rather a matter of relative knowing. National reason is related to human reason as human reason is related to general reason. Each instance of national reason has something that it presents in itself; all else, in contrast, is presented with respect to the way in which human beings in general relate everything with respect to the earth.

(The first task for every distinctive sphere is to find that characteristic whereby the absolute is comprehended in it.)[74]

---

73. Ed. commentary: In 1822 (363f) Schleiermacher explains "nominal definition" more fully but in a way wholly consistent with what is stated here. What arises in this first moment of induction, taken by itself, is merely "an aggregate of signs whereby the relationship of a particular form [or image: *Bild*—but it could be a sound or touch] to a general form is expressed," thus a merely nominal definition not a real one. He explains: "Signs [*Merkmale*— or indicators] are nothing but results of sense perceptual and comparative judgments taken up into the general form. Never is the inner nature of a thing expressed through this definition, for a relation to the intellectual function is lacking. So, only the relationship of objects to the general forms of our organic function is expressed in this definition."

74. Ed. commentary: This recognition of differences of experience between various cultural areas, wherein language comes to affect thinking differentially, is a key point in Schleiermacher's understanding of thinking. Where the will to know is strong, there arises the task of trying to surmount these differences. This latter process amounts to honoring the distinctiveness to be found in each cultural sphere, if for no other reason than that one must do so to be true to the variety of experience and of given meanings, and also attempting to form concepts that truly unite them in some fashion, not that run over them roughshod.

Except perhaps in mathematics, all science, he holds, is obligated to this twofold task. An example of Schleiermacher's own way of working in accordance with the rule he has given in parentheses here is his *Christian Faith*, which basically intends to present only the mode of faith that could then be said to exist among the German Lutheran and Reformed churches at that time and yet also attempts to grasp what is authentically Christian per se ("whereby the absolute is comprehended in it"). One might reasonably add, then, that the more ecumenical (of "the whole inhabited earth"—these days extended to the uninhabited as well) a science becomes, the more likely it is "to find that characteristic whereby the absolute is comprehended in it." Discussion in the following lecture expands on this theme.

Lecture 39

Irrationality is contained not only in nations but also in smaller corporate entities and, indeed, right down to individual persons, only the narrower the sphere the more is that which is *a parte potiori* communal in nature and the less is that which is distinctive in being so.[75]

Now, since only that thinking which is identical in all is knowing, how is this contradiction to be resolved? It is to be resolved with a twofold procedure. The first procedure is to exclude all that is different and let only what is purely identical remain. In this way, only what is absolute remains left at the end. The second procedure is to draw everything together and to extract whatever is irrational through criticism. That is, in the latter way one seeks thereby also to understand the principle of distinctiveness, which views something as a being of itself, and in doing so brings an indirect community of thinking into position.

The two procedures are nothing in isolation from each other. The absolute is nothing without this totality of real knowing wrought by the second procedure, and this totality of real knowing is nothing without that absolute wrought by the first procedure. The identity of that absolute must mediate the totality of real knowing, and the reality of this knowing must fulfill the identity of that absolute.

Now, if relative knowing is not equivalent to error, it does make discovery of error difficult even so. That is to say, as long as I have not understood the principle of a given individuality, I remain uncertain as to whether a bit of thinking that is simply not harmonious is an instance of such individuality or is an error. In an uncertain matter one can proceed only on the basis of presuppositions, and in a twofold fashion. (1) I can view everything to be false that does

---

75. Schleiermacher's note: "It cannot be said that what is distinctive is simply a particular combination and that the concepts involved apply to all alike, for the combination would also be determined along with the concepts, so that the only difference that would remain would be an external one, namely that one does this and another that.

"Depending on how one is disposed, one can say that what is distinctive and relative is grounded only in the organic function or that it is grounded in reason, because in finite perspective reason becomes real only through the organic function and the organic function can produce an actual bit of thinking only through reason.

"The particular that is foreign to me I cannot appropriate; rather, I should reconstruct it in terms of the corresponding foreign concept formation.

"Accordingly, our knowing consists of two factors: pure knowing, which constructs the identity of being and thinking, and critical knowing, which constructs the principles for particular formations of concepts.

"Only in this twofold fashion is it possible to realize the proposition that knowing is a thinking that is identical in all."

not manifestly bear its individual principle with it. (2) I must take everything to be true that does not contradict the absolute rules of thinking.

Lecture 40
(Monday, August 5)

The critical factor is thus an original element of knowing, since it is indispensable already in the earliest form of concept formation.[76] However, real knowing is also something that is never to be brought fully into place. This is so because if the principle regarding what is distinctive as a being of its own, the particular actions of which are but representations, is to be known,[77] this can occur only through the identity of induction and construction,[78] and thus the form of it that comes later is already presupposed in the form of it that has come earlier. Real knowing is also never to be demonstrated with apodictic certainty, because whether things that are really homogeneous have been assembled can be made evident only through their successful issue.[79]

Even the extracting of error can therefore not proceed from this point alone but has still to be started from another point.

---

76. Schleiermacher's note: "This is so, for the principle for forming concepts used by other individuals is already operative on each."

77. Schleiermacher's note: "The task then is to find out of a quantity of given actions the distinctive power that has generated them."

78. Schleiermacher's note: "That is to say, if one has a presentiment of a unity, one must analyze this unity as something general into its particular parts, and if these particular parts are subsequently in agreement with the various moments of induction, surety thus arises."

79. Ed. commentary: Here, as in many other places, the reader may readily have detected major features of pragmatism, which (in comparison with loose adoptions of it by Richard Rorty and some others today) was intended, by Charles Sanders Peirce, William James and John Dewey (as, in effect, earlier by Schleiermacher) to be a carefully laid-out, ever expanding and confident way of getting at "truth," one that can be reliably validated and generally accepted at the time, then further testing one's findings by generally agreed and publicly accessible criteria, reframing one's questions, and continuing this spiral of phases indefinitely. This and other tightly worked-out schemes for conducting inquiry pragmatically are much more demanding and productive than variants on wise sayings like "the proof of the pudding's in the eating," though they do tend always to carry some practical (not necessarily instrumental versus intrinsic) import. Formed in another time and linguistic-cultural area, Schleiermacher's metaphysics and methods come very close, are often identical, to those of these successors—a theme thus far scarcely explored. In addition, there may well be points where Schleiermacher's approach could serve as, or stimulate formation of, a corrective. As examples, James's "pluralism" could be fruitfully corrected by Schleiermacher's ways of handling plurality and distinctiveness along the way to greater, more fully integrated (*vollständige*) wholes and ultimately to the one and all. Dewey's limited definition of science (and thereby of all reflective thinking) as problem solving (usually described in five distinct stages) could easily find correction in Schleiermacher's far more complex, extensive, pragmatically accurate definition of science.

In every action the thing is entirely active and only particular functions come to the fore. In thinking apart from reason the organic function also comes to the fore, and this function has two aspects: an objective one for determination of the object and a subjective one for determination of the situation. Situations too can be assembled and brought under a single concept. Now, if the subjective aspect comes into prominence where it should recede, error has to arise there. In assembly of details the innate system of concepts must be unconsciously active and with it the objective aspect of the organic function. If instead of this process it is the subjective aspect that is active in assembly of details, in this way things are assembled only according to their relation to mere notions, not according to their being. This coming into prominence of personal existence is sin, and error thus arises from sin.[80] Just as on their ethical side human beings only gradually make the transition from sin to virtue, likewise on their theoretical side human beings only gradually make the transition from error to knowledge.

Lecture 41

[First canon:] Error is never absolute. Even relations represented in sensation lead to something that is true, only it is not something by the assembly of which the nature of things is known.

In and of itself, every higher stage in the process of induction is similar to the lowest stage, but correctness and incorrectness can be assigned to their conjoining. Intermediate stages can be leapt over. Thereby the higher concepts become empty, because they do not bear in themselves the living perception of the subordinate circle. This situation arises out of the isolating of induction. One can settle at stages in between that are not real. This is the same thing as the first error. If, in the course of leaping, regularity is what is supplied through further effort, the scheme of knowing still resides in this process;[81] but in the lack of

---

80. Ed. commentary: It may well be a bit of a shock to find error depicted as arising from "sin," though in any case "sin" is not defined theologically here. In a Christian setting Schleiermacher places "sin" solely in connection with "redemption," as "a positive antagonism of flesh against spirit" (*Christian Faith* §66), as in moral terms "a complete incapacity for good" removable only by redemption (§67), "as a disturbance interfering with [our own] nature" (§68), and regarded "in part as based in ourselves ["actual sin"] and in part as based somewhere beyond our own existence" ["original sin"]. Here use of the word "sin" seems to be comparatively metaphorical and refers to the nonmoral side of human life. Thus, where the subjectivity of a person predominates over against the commonality required of knowing, error can easily arise from this sinful disposition. However, as is indicated in the next lecture, not all error arises from this source. In 1814/15 (p. 84) error is referred to as a "sin" of which one can be "guilty" over against a "reflective and self-conscious standpoint."

81. Schleiermacher's note: "If the concept of deity is formed too quickly by means of induction, all that will arise is the concept regarding a most general nature that is devoid of

uniformity this process does not contain the scheme of knowing. The lack of uniformity can also arise simply from the admixing of subjectivity.

The leaping arises from striving upward, because each concept can be fixed only in the identity of the entire series of stages. The second canon is the remedy for such leaping: that one must ever seek to uphold induction's becoming one with construction. This means that one at least seeks to divine for one kind of thing its neighboring kinds and thus to seek in this unity found among them that contrast as one member of which it would have been found by construction. In this way, induction becomes a real preparation for the later process of construction.

Lecture 42

Addenda on induction

1. As to the kind of difference that is successive, a remodeling of concepts becomes necessary when greater interconnectedness arises among particular areas,[82] when one gains greater mastery over the contrasts present there. Even what is surpassed here is not error. For example: (a) regarding the personifying that goes on in the mythical period, there the correct instinct bears no intention of letting the idea of life move onward but it also lacks so far the various forms that would enable this; (b) in the description of nature an entirely different classification is made so long as people as yet have but little information.

2. As to the distinction between a natural and an artificial system of concepts, the first is simply that which is sustained but is not complete, the latter is complete but is merely transitory, proceeding from only one function and corresponding not at all to the natural modification of vital powers.

3. *Addendum to the first canon*: Since no error is absolute and becomes so only by entering into a false series, the canon can also be expressed in the following way, that one should always but remain conscious of whether one is caught up in searching for an instance of being or for an instance of doing and should never confuse either with the other.

4. Do the points of ascent always have to be numerically the same? This question is seen to be unanswerable if one looks at how both determinate and indeterminate plurality are always present in combination.

---

content. Only if one has continually stuck to the identity of induction with construction, thus arriving at contrasts, can this concept turn out well."

82. Schleiermacher's note: "The understanding of any instance of being is composed of its particularity and its being conditioned in relation to all else."

Where a process of strict specification is dominant the points of ascent are also more numerous, whereas where a process of playing dominates less typologizing occurs.

5. *Addendum to the second canon*: In this canon also lies the remedy for the tendency to leap over intermediate stages. If one establishes the maxim of drawing the similarity of details from their distinct forms and not from their general forms, accordingly when one is facing a great mass of details their general similarity would, of course, be presented equally among them, but from this general similarity one would be referred back to the more special similarity. In this respect, within a mass of details differences would likewise be found, which one would at the very least propound as contrasts to be understood on the basis of their higher unity. In this way, the formal features of deduction are likewise inherent in this process of induction and one is engaged in the construction of an instance of true knowing.

Lecture 43

(Monday, August 12)

Concluding remarks on induction:

The two canons set forth are not to be used mechanically. By means of them one can recognize the committing of error, but one will not avoid error if the inner principle of which these canons are the expression is missing. Doing philosophy is an art, because the application of rules cannot in turn be brought under the rules. Rather, such application depends on disposition and talent.

Error is avoided through the clarity and integrity of disposition, which makes what is sense-oriented retreat behind objective interest. Leaping over intermediate stages[83] is avoided through one's love for what is real, which intends to release as little from a given object as is possible, thus as one rises through the various stages sticks with the object as much as possible. To be sure, this love will be able to work only in a distinct area and comprises the actual talent for science.[84] Without it, what we have is merely empty speculation.

If the process of induction is carried out in this way, it must come to an end where deduction begins. Now, since this point consists of the totality of all that lives, one must above all not step outside this domain of all that lives. This end is

---

83. Schleiermacher's note: "In this leap also lies that self-love which would rise as quickly as possible to that higher point at which one who possesses knowledge of the absolute stands above everyone."

84. Schleiermacher's note: "This talent, to be sure, can apply only to a certain circle of objects. Accordingly, there emerges therefrom a proper classification of what is knowable."

reached when everything that has a general nature is seen in turn as something particular, something that cannot persist without its coordinated nature and that is at the same time vitally taken up with its coordinated nature into a higher position. (An example: the ascent from the level of an individual entity through being an animal and being among all that live to being a heavenly body.) This very procedure is grounded in the nature of the concept, which is always an identity of general and particular.

Deduction

On formation of concepts through deduction:

Deduction no more exists without concept formation than concept formation is the first thing that happens, and it is to be considered separately only because deduction does also come to be present as a predominant factor.[85]

As the starting point for deduction the dim consciousness of what is absolute is situated over against the chaotic state of sense perception, taking the form of a tendency that is to be realized precisely through this process, and this is to be done through just such a transition from indeterminate to determinate consciousness. Chaotic sense perception drives us to pursue this indeterminate consciousness of what is absolute, just as indeterminate consciousness of what is absolute drives us to explicate what is perceived. In this way, all knowing is conditioned by the two processes and each process is conditioned by the other. Despite all the organic systems that may exist, without reason there is no material knowing. Despite all the reason that may exist, without organic systems there is no formal knowing.

---

85. Ed. commentary: Compare the final statement in the 42d lecture. Conceptually, the presence of induction and deduction is a matter of more or less. Even though by definition deduction cannot take place unless the premises it uses wholly rely on induction, in an actual process of thinking either one may predominate. In this section, another way of saying that deduction cannot take place unless the premises it uses wholly rely on induction is that the very same two elements that appear in induction—perceptual discrimination and concept formation—become the materials used by deduction, which also consists of two moments, or operations. Its first operation is that of finding a basis for classifying what has been found inductively. Its second operation is to identify a given instance of being both in terms of its internal contrasts and as a unity. Note that below Schleiermacher does use the familiar image of deductive descent, but he uses it only in this respect, moving with additional tools of organization down the scale of forms. In this and other respects, the accounts of induction and deduction are similar in form, though of course different in content. (Compare the somewhat similar account in R.G. Collingwood's *Essay on Metaphysics* (1940) and *Philosophical Method* (1933). Collingwood seems to place greater emphasis on features of a scale, while Schleiermacher seems to place greater emphasis on contrasts found while moving up or down the scale.)

If one posits that there is a differential between the two processes but that deduction also takes its start after induction, the intent of deduction is by moving out of what is united—that is, by forming contrasts—to discover what induction has found by separating things out from the manifold, and in this way the form of contrast moves downward, right down to the particular detail. The dim idea of the absolute and the chaotic manifold belong together in just the same way as do the consummate idea of the absolute and the totality of real knowing.

The process of deduction likewise divides into two moments. A basis for division must be found and a concept of a given being must be constructed that corresponds to the contrast that lies therein and that can be posited in turn as a unity in which some contrast is to be found, thus a sphere of identity between them must be found as well.

Lecture 44

Continuation of the discussion on deduction:

The two moments of deduction are no more to be separated from each other than those of induction. The principle underlying a contrast cannot be definitely posited except in that a division of being is posited at the same time, and no divided being can be thought of than is considered with its basis of division at the same time.

The entire process is best considered in terms of its first beginning. The idea of the absolute is the first member of this process; in it we find the bases of division: being and doing, ideal and real. The relative union of these basic contrasts, or the world, is the second member. The idea of the absolute is unity, what is necessary, what is not directly given; the world is plurality, what is conditioned, what is to be given directly. These characteristics are repeated at each stage. Every member except the first one, the absolute, is an identity of these respective characteristics, because the absolute is the first and last member; as the first member the absolute is supplemented by the totality of what is particular being identical in turn with the absolute.

The question arises: If we abstract from what we know through induction, although it is an earlier instance of knowing, as one must do if one considers just one side of a relative contrast, how must one proceed then to find the basis of division involved? At this stage we do not have the idea of the absolute as the fullness of identity with the consciousness of the contrasts that are dissolved therein; rather, we have that idea as a framework, as a regulative principle. (For the absurdity that appears and is reproved at the outset one sees that there is a moment on which it is based. Yet, in part the idea of the absolute would not be a regulative principle absent its life in us, which is nevertheless only a portion of its eternal reality, and in part this is a point that precedes knowing but is not posited in or through knowing.) If we regard the absolute only in this way and imagine ourselves entirely without any results from induction, it seems as though we have nothing whereby we could form contrasts. (Hence, there is the claim that a philosophy based on the absolute would be a philosophy of nothing.)[86] However, since we ourselves stand under the form of contrast, likewise we do have this idea of the absolute as regulative principle within us; and since all finite consciousness is conditioned by being and doing, ideal and real, and we must also posit a relative identity between the absolute and ourselves, for us the natural basis for division is the scheme that belongs to finite real consciousness. (This original identity of the idea of the absolute and of the form of contrast that is in us constitutes our nature from this aspect. We stand between the absolute and sheer animalization. The absolute lacks the form of contrast, sheer animalization lacks the idea of the absolute.) The idea of the absolute is the ideal germ of thinking; the form of contrast is from the aspect of construction the real germ of thinking. These two contrasts thus return at every single stage. In each case, the higher stage appears as being, the lower as doing (as action of the higher living power), but what is posited in our procedure as a higher member is also posited in turn as being. (Likewise, what is lower is indeed also the predominately real, because it is what is more directly given and will subsequently be viewed in turn from the aspect of what is ideal.)

Lecture 45

Further continuation of the discussion on deduction:

The higher stages are distinguished from the lower stages by the fact that in the higher stages the dyads, simple or complex, dominate, and the deeper one descends the more the next lower level, if one views it as already given, is related to it as an indeterminate plurality, with the result that in its unity no basis for division is to be found. This situation is still no proof, however, that the process of deduction has reached its end and thus that pure science does not reach beyond where it has come up to that point. It is much more likely to be simply a transition point from reflection as being to reflection as doing. For the latter, all the basis for division that is needed is simply a changing "more and less" posited within the higher unity, which "more and less" already lies in the contrast bound

---

86. Arndt note: "The claim that a philosophy based on the Absolute would be a philosophy of nothing refers to Friedrich Koeppen, *Schellings Lehre oder das Ganze der Philosophie des absoluten Nichts* (Hamburg, 1803)."

together within this higher unity. Then, with the help of the other factor, that of action, fixed points are formed that constitute the sphere of the nearest subordinate point. For example, the classes and types of animals are certainly not to be constructed from the idea of animalization other than in this manner.

That what is found in the accomplishment of the process to be doing is, in turn, observed to be being is justified, because the contrast is only a relative one. That people do not keep themselves open to this shift back and forth is an occasion for many misconceptions in natural science. One has before one's very eyes a result gained through induction and then steers arbitrarily so as to attain it through deduction as well. Contrary to this procedure, in the process of deduction every step must be completely justified in terms of the previous step.

The identity of construction and induction at each step consists in induction's being the earlier process by its very nature; as soon as a result is reached through deduction, a concept gained through induction is sought that assuredly corresponds to it. No further progress can be made until that is done.

The following rules are valid for formation of contrast and construction of being that corresponds to that formation:

(1) No contrast may be constructed such that it has a positive and a negative side. If that is done, one has then moved outside the domain of life and no relative union is possible; one would be left with an empty abstraction.

(2) No being is to be posited that would be defined only by one contrast; instead, the identities of all other main contrasts must be included therein. This inclusion is already evident in that at the original level itself we would have found two contrasts that are equally valid in relation to each other. The deeper we descend, the identity of all the more contrasts must be present in each one. Examples of the reverse would be contrasts between mind and matter, considered to be different sorts of being, and onetime elements of an instance of being that was badly constructed.

Note: If in deduction as well one generally goes to what is living, thus to the unity of contrasts, one likewise arrives at indeterminate plurality there. — Or should I have saved this for the process of combination? If I had, however, the deduction involved would be completely abstract. To be sure, one does arrive at the animal and the vegetative, to state and church, by means of dichotomies.[87]

---

87. Ed. commentary: In this lecture Schleiermacher displays his occasional uneasiness about some dichotomies, which may be defined simply as two-membered contrasts, which he primarily meant by the examples he gave, or as two-membered contrasts that are kept rigid or are perhaps kept in tension overlong or overabstractly; and here he also moves more in the

Lecture 46
(Monday, August 19)

Transition to combination:

If the two processes of concept formation are completed in their identity, in this way they present a fully integrated system of perception (for they contain not only the living forms of actions but also their concepts), but as rigid, fixed being and not in an actual living movement.[88] The system produced by combination could then contain nothing but what the system of perception would also contain, but under the form of what is fluid and mobile. In that case, combination is supplementary only by its form; it is that which is genuinely enlivening in its effect.

However, since those two processes are never completed but are always moving toward that status, so much that is not yet given in the process of

---

direction of Collingwood. Both men were no doubt motivated in part by the negative examples of Hegel's own self-styled "logic" (1812-1816), which was set forth as a method for discerning the entire progression of human history and in which each contrast, the two members of which were to be deemed "antithetical" to each other, were eventually to be annulled as such and caught up in, in effect replaced by, a new "thesis" that comprised a "synthesis" of the two. Although Hegel did not come on the Berlin scene until 1818, Schleiermacher was well aware of his published thought and, sometime after Fichte had gone, recommended his appointment there. He did this to his everlasting regret, for Hegel almost immediately went on the attack, viewing Schleiermacher as an enemy, one purveying considerably more liberal, reformist positions politically, philosophically and theologically in comparison with his own more conservative positions. Schleiermacher's popularity among students in Berlin might well have been experienced as threatening to Hegel, thus heightening a separation from each other of both persons. One piece of evidence lies in the fact that in Summer 1822 Hegel lectured on "Logic and Metaphysics" before 74 students, while Schleiermacher had 118 students. In the corresponding lectures in Summer 1828, however, the Hegelian influence had climbed to such an extent that Hegel had 128, Schleiermacher 129 students (Arndt, xxxvi, note 63).

88. In 1814/15, Schleiermacher, now lecturing five times per week on the subject, had already completed 68 lectures of the 70-some hours total up to this point and was beginning a four-hour segment on theory concerning formation of judgment. The second section of the technical part, "On Combination" (comprised of heuristic and architectonic procedures) may have been given short shrift, as here. In 1822, the first section in the "Technical or Formal Part," entitled "Theory of Construction, or the Bringing About of Thinking as Knowing," included a "Preliminary Reflection on the Relative Positions of Knowing and Error" and two subsections on the theory of concept formation (after a brief introduction, it successively treated of the processes of induction and deduction, respectively, much of the latter of which focused on modes of classification) and on the theory of judgment formation. The second section regarded "The Interconnectedness of Knowing: Theory of Combination" and also had two subsections regarding heuristic and architectonic procedures, respectively. This time the transcripts on the second section comprised the final 27 pages.

subsumption can also be materially present in the process of combination. To be sure, judgment does not take place without concept, but the not fully integrated status of perception does not add up to an adequate concept and as such solely goes to the fact that something should be able to enter into a judgment that does so as subject or predicate and that actually has its value here though having no value whatsoever within the process of subsumption.

Now, since the two processes can advance only with each other and mutually condition each other, each process must also be able to be considered of itself.

Combination

On the process of combination:

The incompleted status of induction is the source of incorrect concepts in which the nature of being corresponding to them does not lie but which present the nature of things in an aggregate of particular actions.

The lack of full integration in deduction is the source of incorrect concepts in which the nature of being is presented in an aggregate of negations. (?)[89]

---

89. Ed. commentary: In the 1822 lectures (393–397), Schleiermacher recognizes situations in which "not-x" is a member of a dichotomous or trichotomous contrast. Later (423–428) he performs a critique focused on misguided trichotomous classifications of forms of judgment into problematic, assertorial and apodictic (in which the so-called problematic kind has to drop out), into the categorical, hypothetical and disjunctive (in which the disjunctive is seen not to be comparable to the other two and is also dropped out), and between affirmative, negative and limited (in which the so-called limited sort is taken not to belong). Then he asks: "How can one arrive at the point of making a negative judgment? I can never arrive at this point from the concept of a subject, for this never leads us to what does not belong to it. Thus, the negative judgment never lies directly on the path that the subject takes and likewise not on the path that deduction takes. If I deny a predicate to a given subject, this proceeds from observation of the concept of the predicate (the action). Thus, the negative judgment is nothing but a contribution toward limiting the concept of the predicate. Take, for example, the statement 'Asbestos does not burn'. I cannot arrive at this judgment by observing asbestos, but I can surely do so by way of experiment. If I observe the burning process in its various effects, I arrive in this way at a negative judgment and find here a limitation of this process. The negative judgment has some value only for conditional thinking. If I want to destroy asbestos, I see that I cannot employ the method of burning. I first get into pure thinking, however, only if I know why the asbestos does not burn. Yet, this can be asserted only in an affirmative judgment. The following canon results from such considerations: Every negative judgment is a task that can be fulfilled only by its changing into an affirmative judgment. The negative judgment has its origin in arbitrary thinking or in some incidental sense perception. It is, pure and simple, an individual judgment and must obtain its sanction through the process of deduction."

Judgment rests in the fact that life in finite circumstances calls forth a determinate action of consciousness in the being-in-common of consciousness with the totality of the individual.

Before we have separated out unities from the chaotic totality of individual cases, we perceive actions by our senses. Thus, judgment comes before concept, but subject and predicate are present in every judgment as concepts, and so concept is present before judgment.

The totality of what is finite, when thought of under indeterminate form, is thus the original subject. If the original predicate is to lie outside the subject, it can only be an effect of that same totality of what is finite on the totality of our organic functions. Here subject and object are not yet truly separated from each other, nor are subject and predicate truly separated from each other. (The subject is first to be determined through the various degrees in which a predicate is added to a part of this totality.)

A fully integrated judgment[90] that is expressed through an actual sentence exists only insofar as the process of concept formation has already gained a place and the unities involved are separate. — The fully integrated judgment is twofold in nature: simply to the extent that the fact involved is referred purely to the subject in question and to the extent that this judgment is reduced to two factors. In the latter instance the verb bears its occasion[91] in itself. The first instance is complete and indeterminate, the second is complete and determinate. The first instance is the more general one. Within it lies the possibility of union with all actions and with the form of the predicate. For example, a given person thinks or loves, wherein the entire circle of thinking and loving potentially lies.

Through the plurality of fully integrated judgments one comes to the point of positing the totality of actions[92] as being; one thus comes in turn to an absolute judgment, in which subject and predicate are not definitely separated but behind which the absolute sticks fast. (Is this absolute judgment at the same time the indwelling schematism of cause and effect? Here there is a hovering between the immanent and the transcendent.) — Infinite judgment is comprised of the formal indifference between subject and predicate, because therein the contrast of being and doing is dissolved. Thus, the same thing happens also with respect to the indifference regarding concept.

---

90. *Vollständiges Urteil.*   Ed. note: As below, *vollständig* is one of the words also translated "complete" here; the ones usually found in Schleiermacher's discourse are *vollkommen* or *vollendet.*

91. *Casum.*

92. Schleiermacher's note: "—and this totality, at the same time as the supreme sphere, for complete judgment always moves to form higher spheres."

A concept is certainly abstract to the extent that it has arisen as an element of judgment and, indeed, is put together out of diverse judgments. As soon as such a concept is generated within a system of concept formation it stops being abstract.

Lecture 47

Thus, judgment begins and ends in indifference as between judgment and concept. First, the primitive is the lowest; second, the absolute is the highest; third, the simple is nearer to the primitive and the complex to the absolute. Thus, in progress from the second to the third relation the tendency of the entire form involved is most clearly to be known—that is, what we have here is the formation of a greater sphere. In the concept what is individual is posited as dissolved, as anything existing of itself, through what is universal.

Simple judgment permits of being viewed as presenting a situation solely as an internal fact or also as positing the second factor but as something unknown. In the latter instance it is subsumed under what is complex, in the first instance it is subsumed under what is primitive, because at that point concept formation is still in process (for if it has already reached completion, a general judgment that is not fully integrated is also but an empty one).

Thus, the simple judgment as such represents the separating out of the particular detail from the confused general judgment and leads to the formation of concept. The complex judgment forms a being-in-common and thus refers what is particular back to what is general. This is so, for in this being-in-common particular being is annulled, as it were.

Accordingly, combination has life in general as its aim, insofar as it strives after complex judgment and through this after the infinite.[93] — This broadening tendency, however, is revealed only in synthetic judgments.[94]

---

93. Ed. note: See indexes to his earlier writings for the significance of this term, which basically refers to whatever lies outside the constraints of the finite and thus often bears a religious connotation of the unbounded, the divine.

94. Ed. note: In the 1814/15 lectures on dialectic (p. 111, #79 in the 68th lecture hour) Schleiermacher states: "From this point on, the distinction between analytic and synthetic judgments is viewed as only a relative one." (Kant had made much of this distinction.) He goes on to explain: "That is to say, absolute judgment is in turn an analytic judgment, and all that has preceded it permits of being viewed as preparation for this judgment. However, before the concept of the world is completed no other concept is completed either, thus all other judgments are means to attaining a fully integrated concept and yet are already contained in this one—that is, are analytic. In contrast, the distinction is well-established with respect to every individual subject that is posited of itself, thus nothing is to be taken away from the above proposition." See the next, 48th lecture.

Lecture 48

Closer consideration of the two authentic forms of judgment:

(a) One of the two forms of judgment is that which is not fully integrated. It must be considered as an act wherein the subject is first determined with the predicate, for judgment proceeds from sense perception of the predicate. Empirical error is for the most part false determination of the subject. This error is to be corrected only through sense perception that corresponds to being, or through the second characteristic of knowing. — This form of judgment can be viewed in part as a sheer modification of the subject, in part as something transitive whereby the second factor, however, is X. The latter of the two is alone the truly synthetic judgment. The first occurs even more when the formation of judgment proceeds from pure observation of the subject for the purpose of describing it [accurately].[95]

(b) The second form of judgment is that which is fully integrated. Considered as an act: (a) Often the second factor mentioned just above is posited with the sense perception involved. Then no subject may be put in first place that has not already given itself to be known directly. This is the source of all need to set hypotheses. (b) Both factors may be given indirectly and the relation is uncertain. Then, however, nothing is actually posited as yet, but people often believe peremptorily that something is posited. (c) In some instances the first factor is originally posited (even if it proceeds more from observation of the subject).

Viewed of itself, in every fully integrated, transitive judgment there is a preponderance of one factor that is posited. For this purpose, language has the two forms of active and passive. Relativity does not exactly fit within this schematism. It is based on the fact that every being-in-common is something dissimilar, thus the task there is above all that of determining the apportionment correctly.

Lecture 49

The best means of determining the apportionment correctly is to posit that the given action is a member of an entire sphere from which it must then be more closely determined and that only in terms of this sphere is it at the same time fully known. For example, vegetation is attached to the being-in-common of the earth and sun, adjoining the purest possible action of the earth and the purest possible

---

95. Arndt note: "A word goes here that is indecipherable." Ed. note: A likely word is inserted.

action of the sun, neither of which is ever entirely outside this interconnectedness. This process is, as it were, a referring back to concept formation, so that in every judgment the indifference as between judgment and concept is also present.

Actually no real being-in-common exists without the twofoldness of what is relative. Thus, one must seek its complement in the case of every being-in-common that one posits with some distinct relativity.

Phenomena are in part grounded more through subjects—that is, in individual life—and in part grounded more in the subjects—that is, in life in general. One must not try to throw the two into one class. If one throws everything into the class of life in general, one kills what is individual and subjects are then mere points of transition, operating mechanically. If one throws everything into the class of individual life, one kills the interconnectedness, operating magically.

Note: The conflict that comes up in the forty-eighth hour, as to which judgment is placed higher, that which is immanent or that which seeks after the other factor mentioned, probably belongs earlier, at the beginning.

CONCLUSION
[From Twesten's Transcript][96]

96. These lectures apparently ended on or about August 26, 1811. See Jonas's summary from a student's notes, of the conclusion to these lectures, which Jonas mistakenly assigns to a 50th rather than a 49th hour, in SW III.4:2 (1839), p. 361. Arndt (p. 61f) appends this conclusion from Twesten's notes. No actual conclusion is in evidence in the notes from 1811 or 1814/15. In 1822 the lectures end with an eight-page account (456–464) of architectonic procedures for "combination," in which the very last question considered concerns the relationship between dialectic and mathematics. The general answer is that in dialectic we have to do with what is general but is at the same time with what is individual, because that goes back to what can occur in individual consciousness. In reverse, in mathematics the individual object is considered—moreover, as an immediate construction in time and space—but only in the form of what is general.

As is "generally recognized but not yet definitely articulated," claims Schleiermacher (463f): "In every real instance of knowing that intends to be an instance of pure thinking and thus to come close to the idea of knowing and through the architectonic procedures is supposed to form a science in its interconnectedness with other sciences, there is only so much truly permeative knowing as contains dialectic and mathematics within it." Yet, a certain onesidedness, he further claims, must be overcome if that near approach to knowing is to be achieved. "That is to say, certain people will say that mathematics, viewed as critical principle, stands in a closer relationship to physical science and likewise dialectic to ethical [human] science. However, this view is an illusion. These people confuse content and form in the belief that physical science belongs more to the empirical form and ethical science more to the speculative form. The truth is that mathematics is more closely allied to the empirical form, dialectic more allied to the speculative form. If thinking is considered as an act from its purely temporal side, it moves into the constructive work of mathematics, for I must appraise how much truth and error lies in it, wherewith it is thus concerned with a purely quantitative relationship. I must also search for its genetic coefficients so as to have knowledge about how a given thought has emerged, and this mathematical matter must generally be correctly affirmed at the outset. In contrast, it is always the case that a speculative natural science can be set forth only according to dialectical principles, in that it thereby arrives at proper construction and particularly at the contrast between being-posited-of-itself and being-posited-with-each-other. As a consequence, one arrives at the empirical and thus moves into the domain of mathematics."

Contrary to Plato's view, Schleiermacher avers, mathematics is not a prerequisite for starting to obtain philosophical knowledge, Schleiermacher continues. Rather, mathematics comes onto the scene once thinking is treated technically and in the light of confusions that have arisen in it, so as "to order thinking in a well-defined manner." Moreover, "this ordering

Everything belongs to the aspect of judgment formation that concerns determination of the subject. It remains to set up the predicate. Actually, that part belongs in the sphere of subsumption. If the concept is established, then every judgment is a subsumption of the particular fact under that concept. Yet, precisely here a particular error is possible, namely one that arises through confusion of the objective with the subjective. In its primitive form, this confused situation is not yet thoroughly sorted out. The pure separation of the two can thus also take place overall only with progress in knowing. In the organic function that underlies a judgment, originally a modification of the organ is predicated, the result of a being-in-common of the organ and the object involved. Thus, it must first be established what the function of the object is in an event; otherwise one posits the subjective instead of the objective. If one has not yet been able to decide, one must take up the preliminary judgment into the judgment that is made concerning the object. In the object something has preceded that, along with what proceeded from my organ, has generated this effect (for example, jaundice). At that point, we come back in turn to the fact that only a continuing control of that which the organic function effects in a person can generate a fully integrated instance of knowing. So, the task of forming a judgment is complicated in itself; just as no concept can be formed

---

is the fruit of mathematics, for only at that point can dialectical procedure begin, and without mathematics it is difficult to awaken consciousness. Plato's claim simply goes to the natural succession of knowledge in every individual person. In every instance of knowing, there is only so much true knowing and so much knowing permeated in accordance with its idea as dialectic and mathematics are present in it—that is to say, dialectic to the degree that it appertains to speculative form and mathematics to the degree that it appertains to empirical form. The two do not permit of being separated, if we do not want to lose knowing itself. The character of knowing is grounded only in their joining and ever stronger interpenetration. This last statement is the general canon for all sciences, if people's will is to value and advance them." Thus does Schleiermacher close his 1822 lectures on dialectic.

There is another important matter belonging to a conclusion, to which Schleiermacher summarily adverts near the end of the 1814/15 notes (p. 110f). There he indicates "the dependence of dialectic on hermeneutics, which is in turn also dependent on dialectic." This interdependence, which makes his accounts of hermeneutics a twin to those of dialectic, will be taken up in a companion volume on hermeneutics. It is highly significant in the light of this relationship between the two areas, one on thinking as knowing and the other on thinking as interpretation, and their corresponding arts, that each investigation arose for Schleiermacher in the light of two trends, which have far from disappeared even today. The first trend is to exempt religious inquiry and presentation from the general requirements of science and interpretation, respectively. The second trend is to import religious notions into either speculative or empirical aspects of both science and interpretation where they do not belong, thus missing the connections that are really, appropriately there. In these terms, religion still represents a very important set of issues that needs attending to in these two interdependent areas of thinking.

without having recourse to other concepts, so no judgment can be formed without having recourse to other judgments.

Judgments are divided into general, particular and individual. If I form a particular object into the subject of a predicate and posit an individual object, in that way I get a pure individual judgment ("A hates B"). In contrast, I can also posit an aggregate of several homogeneously posited things as a subject. Actually, there is always a correspondence to any such judgment of another judgment to which a different predicate is adjoined. Finally, I can also posit an individual as subject without determining the second factor, and then the judgment is also a general one, since it is not an individual fact that is predicated but an entire sphere—the situation is similar if I predicate something of a totality without determining the second factor. What significance do these various judgments have?

Manifestly, every particular judgment refers to a separation; here the intention is to form an intermediate concept between the unity involved and the particular detail, and thus the particular judgment lies within the process of concept formation. General judgment too intends to give definition to the concept. If the second factor is not posited, I view the predicate solely as a state of the thing and not in its temporal character but as a capacity or living impulse that necessarily belongs to its nature. If, in contrast, I have constructed the concept in its fully integrated form already, this is no judgment. The particular individual judgment, however, specifically includes the act of combination in itself, removes the existence-of-itself of the individual and places it in its identity with what is general. Hence, general judgments of the second kind might be viewed as particular judgments, as, for example, in the statement "plants love the light." Here I proceed out of a small sphere and seek the greater, the being-in-common of plants and light; what is involved is what is internal not to the plants but to a greater sphere, that of vegetative life and light together. Every particular judgment moves toward such extension, and so it is simply the actual judgment that serves concept formation no longer but supplements it. — In the process of judgment it is necessary always to remain conscious of its standpoint. If one does not have the relationship to the concept in view, the process will easily become defective. This consciousness, however, will be maintained if one is conscious of the form in which one constructs the judgment.

The details can now easily be further developed on the analogy of what has already been done. This will show that transcendental and formal knowing belong tightly together and that without each other they are nothing.

BIBLIOGRAPHICAL NOTE

Essays on Schleiermacher's dialectic in the forthcoming volume V of *New Athenaeum/Neues Athenaeum* refer to much of the literature on this subject of special interest to date. The first book focusing on the dialectic texts in English is Thandeka's thought-provoking critical work *The Embodied Self: Friedrich Schleiermacher's Solution to Kant's Problem of Empirical Self* (Albany: State University of New York Press, 1995), xiv, 151 p. An important complementary article by David E. Klemm on "Dispute, Dialogue, and Individuality in Schleiermacher's *Dialektik*" appears in *New Athenaeum/Neues Athenaeum* volume IV (1995), originally presented at the American Academy of Religion meetings in 1991. With respect to a different set of problems, these recent investigations were preceded by John E. Thiel, *God and World in Schleiermacher's Dialektik and Glaubenslehre: Criticism and the Methodology of Dogmatics* (Bern: Lang, 1981), xiv, 239 p. My own early study on *Schleiermacher's Theological Method* (Princeton Theological Seminary Dissertation, 1961) made use of the dialectic material but only in a comparatively minor way.

Many works to be contended with in German include Eilert Herms, *Herkunft, Entfaltung und erste Gestalt des Systems der Wissenschaften bei Schleiermacher* (Gütersloh: Gerd Mohn, 1974), 285 p.; Falk Wagner, *Schleiermachers Dialektik: Eine kritische Interpretation* (Gütersloh: Gerd Mohn, 1974), 288 p.; Hans-Richard Reuter, *Die Einheit der Dialektik Friedrich Schleiermachers* (München: Christian Kaiser, 1979), 290 p.; and Michael Eckert, *Gott—Glauben und Wissen: Friedrich Schleiermachers Philosophische Theologie* (Berlin: de Gruyter, 1987), xii, 227 p. All four works are by philosopher-theologians, and their books are products of graduate study. The same is true of Thandeka, Thiel and Tice.

Essays in German by Peter Weiß, Sergio Sorrentino and Michael Eckert appeared in *Schleiermacher in Context*, ed. by Ruth Drucilla Richardson (Lewiston, N.Y.: Edwin Mellen Press, 1991), 203–226, 227–241, 421–441. In Italy, Sergio Sorrentino's publications have led the way among several authors writing on Schleiermacher's dialectic primarily in that language. Andreas Arndt, a member of the Schleiermacherforschungstelle in Berlin who has written much on the subject and has already edited the 1811 and 1814/15 notes, the 1833 introduction and allied materials in two small volumes for Felix Meiner Verlag (Hamburg, 1986, 1988), contributed an essay "Zur Vorgeschichte des Schleiermacherschen Begriffs von Dialektik" to *Schleiermacher und die Wissenschaftliche Kultur des Christentums*, hg.v. Günter Meckenstock (Berlin & New York: Walter de Gruyter, 1991), 313–334.

Developments in the literature may be followed in a series of bibliographies published by me. The first two are, regrettably, out of print, but a comprehensive compilation is being planned. They were published by Princeton University Press in cooperation with Princeton Theological Seminary. The ongoing updates are appearing in *New Athenaeum/Neues Athenaeum*, so far in volumes 1 (1989), 280–350, 2 (1991), 131–163, and 4 (1995), 140–194. Try libraries for *Schleiermacher Bibliography: With Brief Introductions, Annotations and Index* (1966), 168 p., and *Schleiermacher Bibliography (1784–1984): Updating and Commentary* (1985), 119 p., plus a nine-page insert, *Schleiermacher Bibliography: Corrections, New Information and Comments* (1985).

INDEXES

As with other texts by Schleiermacher that I have edited, my aim has been to represent the precise meanings and details of his discourse, first in the notes (n) but especially in the indexes. Here the entries are numerous for such a short piece, reflecting the great density of these preparatory notes. I trust the care I have taken will prove fruitful for beginning readers as well as scholars wishing to trace conceptions and judgments, arguments and comparisons, allusions and references here. Already enough of such close attention to the details has been given to enable close in-depth study across texts. Since a great many entries require not only references to the original German but philosophical clarity as to Schleiermacher's meanings and intentions, for the most part no mechanical procedure could ever produce such indexes.

NAMES AND PLACES

SUBJECTS AND CONCEPTS

A parte potiori, 58

A priori and a posteriori (empirical), 5n, 33, 46

Absolute, the absolute, what is absolute (*Absolute, absolute*), xv, xvi, xviii, xxiii, 2n, 10, 11, 27, 35, 38, 41n, 64; as a framework, regulative principle, 64–65; as God, deity, Supreme Being, 24; as the highest, 70; as transcendent idea, 24n; as what is necessary, 64; becoming vs. being, 24n, 26, 29n; being, 33–34, 39; consummate idea of, 64; contrast and, 65; dim consciousness (idea) of, 63, 64; eternal reality of, 65; fundament of all thinking, 39; having it as reason, xxii, 38; idea of, 40, 64; idea of as the real germ of thinking, 65; identity of being and doing, 35; identity of concept and object in, 27, 41; identity of thinking and being in, 39; in the particular, 50; its life in us, 65; knowledge of the, 62n; not a singular thing, 31; predication, 26; present in form, 40; re: God and world, 39–41; relative identity between it and ourselves, 65; religious form of, 40; source of all real knowing, 22n; standing under the form of identity, 43; terminus of historical process, 37n; transcendent as, 38; ultimate unity, 36; unconscious idea of, 40; unity of the, 28, 64; upward to the, 49; world and, 43, 64

Abstract (*abstract*), 66, 70

Absurdity (*Verkehrtheit*), 43; (*Absurdität*), 64

Accidental (*zufällig*), 2n; vs. essential, 39

Acknowledge (*anerkennen*), 8, 29

Act (*Act*), 71, 73n, 75; (*That*), 33

Action (*Action*), 51, 52n, 53–55, 59, 60, 66; and reaction (*Reaction*), 46; individual, 50, 51, 53; living forms and concepts of, 67; negates space, 46; of consciousness, 69; of earth and sun, 71; thinking as, 41, 42. *See also* Doing

Action (*Handeln, Handlung*), 22, 22n, 32, 33, 35; in common, 34; self-initiated,

36n; totality in each, 35; totality of all, 34, 69

Activity (*Thätigkeit*), 8, 9 ,50, 52n, 54, 55; (*Activität*), 33, 34n

Actuality (*Wirklichkeit*), 44

Affection, organic, 30n

Agathon, 6, 6n

Aggregate (*Aggregat*), 38, 56, 68; posited as a subject, 75

Allgemeine, das höchste, 4n

Analogous, analogy, 14n, 15, 53, 75

Analogue(s), of knowing, 8, 13

Anerkennen, see Recognition

Animalization (*Animalisation*), 65–66

Anschauung, see Perception

Antithesis (*Entgegensetzung*), 8, 44, 67n

Apportionment (*Antheil*), 71

Appropriate (*aneignen*), 58n

Arbitrary (*willkührlich*), arbitrariness (*Willkührlichkeit*), 3, 7, 16n, 17, 40, 41, 41n, 47, 66, 68n; essential vs., 32; every concept, 25; not proceeding from being, 17

Architectonic, 67n, 73n

Area, see Domain

Art (*Kunst*), 4; levels of, 3n; medium of, 4; of doing philosophy (*see also* Dialectic); science and, 3n; work of, 4, 13n

Artificial (*kunstlich*), 61

Assertion, assert (*Behaupten, Behauptung; behaupten, aussagen*), 1n, 2n, 20, 22; assertorial judgment, 68n. *See also* Claim

Assumption, 2n, 9. *See also* Supposition

Astronomy, 43n

Asymptotes, xviii, 52

Atheism, 32

Axioms, 46, 47

Becoming (*Werden*), 24n, 26, 29n, 33; knowing as, 31. *See also* Being

Being (*Sein*), xi, xv, xvi, 29, 65; absolute, xv, 33, 41; all exists in what is absolute, 34; and doing, 56, 61, 64–66; as posited in thinking, 16; at the lowest level, 30; being common to (*gemeinsames Sein*), 32; being-of-itself of

Definition (*Definition*), 46–47; axioms based on, 46; nominal, 57, 57n

Deity, xx, 39; as absolute, 24n; concept of via induction, 60n; idea of, 29n, 32, 39; image of, xxiii, 31; knowledge of, the basis of all knowledge, 31; no isolated perception of, 31; principle of all being, xxii, 38; transcendent being and idea, xxii, 38; vital foundation of all process, xxiv; vital perspective on the, xxii, 38. *See also* God

Demonstration (*Demonstration*), 29

Departure (point of), 50

Dependence, on a single higher being and thinking, 39

Description, 22n, 71; of nature, 61

Determinate, determined, definite, definition given to, distinct (*bestimmt*), 25, 26, 36, 53, 64, 69, 71, 72, 75; indeterminate subject, 52n, 53; manifoldness, 30; self-, 53

Development (*Entwicklung*), free, xxi, human, xvi; of historical phenomena, xx; of truth, xix

Dialectic, xii, 37n, 73n–74n; absolute in, 24n–25n, 37n; against lower-level reflection, 5n; architectonic for the principles of science, 1; art of doing philosophy, ix, xi, 1n, 3, 7, 62; as a science, 1n, 3n, 7; as a work of art, 14n; as dialogue, 6; as general organon of all science, 1n, 7; as highest (supreme) art, 4, 14n; as supreme and most general knowing, 6; as the primary philosophical discipline, 7n; definition of, xiv, 1n, 3, 3n, 6, 7n; formal, technical aspect, 44n–45n (*see also* transcendental below); in relation to physics and ethics, 1n, 5n, 6 (*see also* Ethics, Physics); interdependence with hermeneutics, 74n; leading to physics throughout, 29; mathematics and, 73n–74n; skepticism no harm to, 8; theology and, 77; transcendental and formal in, xiv, xxiv, 2n, 10, 11, 33, 34, 36n, 37n, 38, 41, 75 (belong tightly together). *See also* Architectonic, Combination, Heuristic

Dialectic lectures, 67n, 78; all years, xxiin; 1811: ix, xi, 1n, 73n, 78; 8–10th, xvii; 11th, xviii; 15th, xxiii; 17th, xxiii; 18th, xxii; 13d, xxii; 24–25th,

xxiii; 33d, xviii; 39th, xviii; 43d, xvii; 48th, 70n, 72n; 1814/15: xxiin, 2n–4n, 14n, 30n, 49n, 70n; 1822: xiv, 57n, 67n, 73n–74n; 1831: xi; 1833: xxiin, 2n, 78

Dialogue, xii, 6, 7n; *I and Thou*, 6n

Dichotomy (*Dichotomie*), 66, 66n, 68n (also trichotomy)

Difference (*Differenz*), 58n, 62

Dignity (*Dignität*), 10

Discriminations, 37n, 51n; perceptual, 63n

Disposition (*Gesinnung*), xxi, 6n, 62

Dispute (*Streit*), xii, 6n; as lively conversation, 6n

Distinctive, distinctiveness (*eigenthümlich, Eigenthümlichkeit*), xviii, 17n, 34, 37n, 57, 57n, 58, 58n, 59, 59n; principle of, 50, 58

Divine, as unbounded, 70n. *See also* Deity, God

Division (*Theilung*), 64. *See also* Classification

Doing (*Thun*), 33, 56, 64, 65, 69. *See also* Act, Action, Activity

Domain(s), sphere(s), area(s), region(s) (*Gebiet, Sphäre*), 14n, 34, 57, 62, 69; aesthetic, 14n; of formal elements, 21; of knowing, xxii, 38; of life, xix–xxv, 62, 66; of morality and reason, xxii; of organic elements, 21; of real knowing, 42; transcendent over ethical and physical, 23. *See also* Sphere

Dualism, duality, God-matter, 39–40; mind-body, 15n

Dyads (*Dyas*), 65

Earth, 45, 57; being-in-common of sun and, 71; bound to the, 43, 44n; people of the, 43n

Ecumenical, 57n

Eidos, 29, 29n

Empirical, the, xiv, xviii, xx, 3, 23, 27, 33, 54n, 55, 73n–74n; consciousness, 56; error, 71; heuristic, 46; mathematics more closely allied to the empirical form than ethics, 73n

Empirical views, empiricism, 27, 28, 44n; trial-and-error, 45n

Eristic, 6, 10

Erkennen, see Cognition

Idea(s) (*Idee*), associations of, 54n; concept and, 28–29, 52n; exchange of, 7; no detail can entirely correspond to its, 8; of life, 61; theory of, 28, 29n; theory of innate, 30n (*see also* Concept); transcendent, 24n

Idea, 29, 29n

Ideal, the (what is), xv, 42, 64, 65

Idealistic views, idealism, xx, 27; absolute idealism, xxiii; hovering between cognition and invention, 28; purely speculative, xxi. *See also* Realistic views

Identity, xvii–xviii; absolute standing under the form of, 43; among contrasts, xv; between a higher and lower concept, xxiii; completion of, 52; dissolution of judgment, xvii; equivalence (in math), xvii; fullness of, 64; in the knowing of all persons, xvii, 7n, 19n, 57; indistinguishability, xviii; inseparable, xvii; not necessarily one or at one, xvii; of a single entity, xviii; of being and concept, 31; of being and doing, 56; of being and knowing, 27; of concept and judgment, 25, 35; of being and nonbeing, 24n, 26; of being and thinking (reason), 16n, 17, 23, 39, 41; of concept and judgment, 22; of concept and thing (object), 23, 27, 39, 43; of concept formation and induction, 54; of general and individual factors, 15, 51, 52, 63; of induction and construction, 56, 59, 61, 66; of main contrasts, 66; of principles and procedures, 7n; of sense perception and construction, 28; of thinking in all, 58; self-, 32; sphere of (*Identitätsphäre*), 64

Ignorance, xix

Imagine, imagination (*einbilden, einsehen*), 8

Immortality, xx

Impulse (*Trieb*), 75

Indicators (*Anzeigen*), 55

Indifference (*Indifferenz*), 69, 70

Individual (*Einzelnes, einzeln*), 15, 23, 25, 26, 27, 29, 32, 33, 35, 38, 44, 53, 56; act of thinking, 50; being of, 30; existence-of-itself (*für sich bestehen*) of, 75; judgment, 75; other, 59n; something, 51; totality of, 69

Individual, what is (*individuelle, individuale*), 4n, 14n, 50, 70, 72

Individuality (*Individualität*), 53, 58

Individuum, 15n

Induction, 43, 44, 45n, 54–63, 67n; and deduction, 62, 63, 63n, 64; as the result of organic function, 44; ascent in, 61–63; identity of construction and, 56, 59, 61, 66; incomplete status of, 68; leaping over intermediate stages of, 60–62; moments of, 59; stages of, 60–61

Infinite, 4, 70

Information (*Kenntnis, Kenntnisse*), 1n, 2n, 7, 9; lack of, 61; real, 42

Inquiry, xxiv, 6n, 37n, 59n; field of, xiv

Insight (*Einsicht*), 31

Instinct (*Instinct*), 50, 61

Integrated, fully, see *Vollständig*

Intellectual function, 57n. *See also* Organic function

Interconnection, connection, interconnectedness (*Zusammenhang*), xvi, 6n, 7, 17n, 41n, 44n, 61, 72; of all knowing, 4n; of nature, xxi, 22n; of the subject's states, xx

Interest, 7, 22, 62

Interpretation, 74n. *See also* Hermeneutics

Intuition, 18n; *see also* Perception

Invention (*Dichten*), and cognition, 28

Investigation (*Untersuchung*), 4, 15; concerning form, 44; in dialectic, 10, 16n, 18; into being, 16n; scientific, 14n

Irrationality (*Irrationalität*), xix, 58

Is, xvii. *See also* Being, Existence

Judgment(s), xiii, 21n, 22n; absolute, 69, 70, 70n; affirmative, 68n; analytic vs. synthetic only a relative distinction, 70n; as combination, 22; as discriminations, 22n; as identity of subject (being) and predicate (nonbeing), 25; as instance of knowing, 32; assertorial, 68n; complex, 70; concepts and, xvii, 22, 24n, 25, 32, 35, 36, 36n, 46n, 50–51, 68, 69, 72, 74; consisting of subject and predicate, 25–26, 32; contrast belonging to, 23; formation of, 31–33, 49, 67n, 74; fully integrated, 69, 70; general (*allgemeine*), particular (*besondere*) and individual (*einzelne*),

Perception, perceptiveness, perspective, perceive (*Anschauung, anschauen*), xxi, 16n, 18n, 20; always more in mind than we perceive, 50; at different levels of mentation, xix; collective system of, xxiii, 31; feeling and, xix, xxv; fully integrated system (status) of, 67, 68; higher, 28; living, 60; of an action, 55; of God, deity, xxiii, 5, 31, 38; of inner sensibility, 22; of knowing, 49; of pleasure, 22; of the universe, 18n; of the world, 31–32; on time and space, 46; vs. sheer formal thinking, 19n; within ourselves, 13n. *See also* Organic, Sense perception

Personal existence (*Persönlichkeit*), 13n, 14n, 15; coming into prominence of as sin, 60; mediation through, 15

Personifying (*Personificiren*), 61

Phenomenon, appearance (*Erscheinung*), 29n, 40, 44n, 72

Philosophers, ancient (Greek), xii, xiv, xv, 6, 10; Enlightenment, xviii; fifteenth century, xiv

Philosophy, xiv, xvi; and history, 36n; death of, 6; doing (*philosophiren*: philosophizing), 3n–4n, 4; knowing in, 31; of history, 37n; philosophical cognition, 33; requires scientific investigation, 14n; religion and, xix; science and, xiv, 3n; system building in, 44; the supreme science, 3n; theism as triumph of, 29n; transcendental and formal the same, 1n, 5, 10. *See also* Dialectic, Philosophers

Physics, 5n, 29n, 31n; time and space in, 46. *See also* Ethics, Science

Piety, xxi

Pleasure, and the lack of it, 22

Plurality (*Vielheit*), 56, 59n, 69; indeterminate, indistinct, 31, 53, 54, 61, 65, 66

Poetic, 7n

Polemic, 41

Positing, posited (*setzen, gesetzt*), 15, 20, 30, 56, 64, 66, 70, 70n, 71, 74; a being independent of knowing, 16n, 18n; absolute, 39, 41; being and knowing as comparable, 27; being-posited-of-itself and with-each-other, 73n; child's of itself, 51; concept and judgment as

independent, 50; in materialism, 40; mutually of idealistic and empirical outlooks, 27; of a subject, 24n, 25–26, 70n, 75; of a thing and of an action, 55–56; of being in judgment, 32; of less nonbeing, 28; of nature, 16n; of reason as a kind of being, 18; of space and time, 46; of the absolute, 65; of unity of concept and object, 41; preliminary, 55; provisional, 56; the totality of actions as being, 69; unity and contrast, 64

Postmodern, xvi, 17n

Power(s) (*Kraft*), distinctive generating given actions, 59; higher living, 65; of speculation, 10; vital, xxiv, 61. *See also* Force

Practical affairs, 8n

Pragmatism, xvi, 59n

Predicate(s), xvii, xviii, 24n, 25, 27, 32, 35, 51–52, 68, 71, 75; false, 17; original, 69; setting up the predicate, 74

Presentation (*Darstellung*), 4, 7, 13n, 27, 29

Presentiment (*Ahndung*), 59

Presupposition (*Voraussetzung*), xii, xiv, xxv, 9, 20, 29, 32; in uncertain matters, 58; mutual between concept and judgment, 22, 23. *See also* Copositing, Positing

Primitive (*primitive*), 70, 74

Principles, xii, 2n; constitutive and regulative, 5, 64; dialectical, 73n; first, 3; for dialogue, 6; for doing philosophy, 5; for forming concepts, 59; of construction, 10; of induction, 62; supreme principles, 8–10

Problems, xv; problem solving in science, 59n; so-called problematic judgment, 68n

Procedure (*Verfahren*), 10, 43, 55n, 58, 63, 65, 66, 73n

Production (*Production*), 30; productive power, 31, 53

Productivity (*Productivität*), 30

Progression, xvi

Proposition (*Satz*), 7, 70n

Providence, xxiv

Psychology, 15n

Puzzles, xv